THE NOONDAY DEVIL

THE NOONDAY DEVIL

DEVIL

Spiritual Support in Middle Age

by

BERNARD BASSET, S.J.

ACADEMY GUILD PRESS
FRESNO, CALIFORNIA

© Bernard Basset, 1964

FIRST AMERICAN EDITION

LIBRARY OF CONGRESS CATALOG CARD NUMBER: 64—25723

DE LICENTIA SUPERIORUM ORDINIS
NIHIL OBSTAT: HUBERTUS RICHARDS, S.T.L., L.S.S.
CENSOR DEPUTATUS
IMPRIMATUR: GEORGIUS L. CRAVEN
EPISCOPUS SEBASTOPOLIS
VIC. CAP.
WESTMONASTERII: DIE 9a MAII 1963

The Nihil obstat *and* Imprimatur *are a declaration that a book or pamphlet is considered to be free from doctrinal or moral error. It is not implied that those who have granted the* Nihil obstat *and* Imprimatur *agree with the contents, opinions or statements expressed.*

LITHOGRAPHED AND BOUND IN THE UNITED STATES OF AMERICA

TO
R. AND J. W.
FOR SO MUCH KINDNESS
OVER SO MANY YEARS

CONTENTS

ACKNOWLEDGEMENTS

I AM grateful to Siegfried Sassoon, C.B.E., for permission to reproduce the sonnet on p. 34, and to the following publishers for permission to quote from the books mentioned: Messrs Sheed & Ward (*Theology and Sanity* by Frank Sheed), Messrs Faber & Faber (*Reason and Emotion* by Professor John Macmurray), Messrs Chatto & Windus and Messrs Harper & Row, New York (*The Perennial Philosophy* by Aldous Huxley), and to Messrs Benziger Brothers, Inc., New York, holders of the copyright of *Difficulties in Life* by Rudolph Allers.

B. B.

FOREWORD

THE Noonday Devil is mentioned in the 90th psalm. He was one of the hazards about which we prayed during Sunday compline before modern scholars improved the translation and despatched him to where he belongs.

We may mourn his passing, for he stood for the trials and temptations which may assail us after our youthful fervour has faded and before we enjoy the peace and resignation of old age. There are temptations peculiar to middle age—fear, guilt, lack of fervour and loss of conviction—and the Noonday Devil seemed to our fathers an apt trade-mark for this middle-aged brand of discouragement.

This book carries the Noonday Devil on its title-page because it will busy itself with the problems of middle age. The author, having lived for many years with himself and others, is fully aware of such discouragement. He now recognizes the need for much spiritual adjustment as the soul on its journey towards eternal happiness passes from A.M. to P.M. Without such adjustment we may begin to judge ourselves too severely and for the wrong motives; we may even retard our spiritual maturity through a lack of awareness of God's abiding love.

He would be a naïve and very foolish writer who would persuade himself that readers pay any great attention to the Foreword of a book. Yet, certain clear warnings must be given somewhere to save the reader

ix

disappointment at a later stage. This book is not intended for every type of reader but for those only who
have met the Noonday Devil in one or other of his
many forms. Again, so small a book cannot pretend to
offer the whole or even the major part of the story of
God's love for us. Where St Francis de Sales wrote an
introduction to the devout life, here is but an introduction to an introduction with a section at the back—part
bibliography, part index—for the sake of those who
may wish to read further for themselves.

The author has in mind a simple book for middle-aged
folk, lying between the age groups of eighteen and
eighty, who are puzzled by the social and economic
upheavals of our days. Some, like himself, may have
suffered the sorrows of two world wars. Others may
have found that their very faith has been rustled by the
wind of change blowing so strongly even from the
direction of Rome. It is the author's hope that he may
help to lighten the burden by showing that the love
of God rides high above the tensions of any particular
age. Here is his aim and to further it he has deliberately
omitted any topic, however holy or however helpful,
which might obscure this central theme. Even with the
subjects treated, he has gone no further than seemed to
him necessary. This very superficiality may help those
who are not themselves experts and who might shy
away from any more expert account.

Need it be said that no uncharity is intended in the
asides, the quips, the many irrelevances which may
seem to disgrace this book. Principally the author is
laughing at himself. He has discovered that in middle
age we grow steadily worse while we long more and
more ardently to get better and that the soft light

from our incipient haloes plays first on the straws in our hair.

Two nuns, two priests, a teacher, a nurse, a mother and a Brigadier kindly read through the rough copy of this book. Theirs was a thankless task and the author has tried to thank them by adopting most of their suggestions and requests. He must return thanks to kind friends in St Ives, Wareham, Newcastle and Bournemouth who bore with him during the long and painful exercise of sticking out his neck.

Bournemouth
November 1963

1

SETTING THE STAGE

HERE is a cheerful book on a mildly morbid subject, for few much care for the thought of middle age. Happily the boundaries are ill defined and may be shifted forwards and backwards to allow to each reader the benefit of every doubt. Only the young, in fact, want middle age to come more quickly to free them from the tyranny of patronage. "Damn it all, Dad; I'm nearly twenty!" is the plea of young men and women, the world over, who long to be taken seriously. As far as this book is concerned all readers between the ages of eighteen and eighty may qualify as middle-aged if they so wish.

The older we grow, the more we seek to push the frontier backwards in the hope of remaining reasonably young for a few more years. Indeed, present society forces us to do so with its heavy emphasis on youth. Other epochs paid greater respect to age and wisdom for, with many dying younger, both these commodities were in short supply. Gone are the glorious days of Solomon when the matriarch could deck out her old man in all his finery and seat him among the elders at the city gate. Today he must be off each morning if he is to hold his job. As it grows increasingly hard to find employment after forty, we must all try to remain at thirty-five for as long as we can. So some lie about their age, others rely on massage, pills and beauty preparations, thus hoping to fool others by almost deceiving

I

themselves. When all other hope has gone, they fall back on a cliché, consoling themselves that a man is only as old as his arteries. Thus they disguise the approach to the last ditch.

TWO ATTITUDES TO MIDDLE AGE

In facing middle age, there are two approaches from which to choose. The first is designed for those who accept no other world than this one and who must, therefore, fulfil themselves inside the allotted span. Twenty precious years are wasted in adolescence and rheumatism may well snatch away another ten at the other end. Forty years remain for adult satisfaction if life, as it is presented to them by the Sunday papers, is to be attained. One failure in love, one slip in finance, one missed opportunity and there may be no chance to start again. With time so short, it is not surprising that life after forty becomes as hectic as the last week of the holidays. Nor is it strange that those who have missed their opportunity carry a lasting grievance with them to the grave.

The religious man of any faith—I am not now thinking of Catholics or churchgoers—must take the second and opposite view of middle age. He must surely believe that he is not as old as his arteries but as young as his soul. Spiritually there is no such period as middle age. A very different system of counting applies for those who accept eternity, for whom a seventieth birthday is very much nearer to the beginning than to the end. The soul does not age. It wears no wrinkles, its voice is not tremulous, it carries itself with more assurance at seventy than at seventeen. It is possible to grow more magnanimous, more wise, more tolerant as year follows year.

If we study these two attitudes to life, we may notice that the pattern of behaviour will vary greatly according to our choice. Pagan life has followed the same order throughout history. From youthful ambition comes the scramble for power, the search for security, the struggle with rivals, eventual surrender and stoical resignation in the end. William James quotes Marcus Aurelius on this for the lofty stoicism of the great Roman Emperor is typical of the highest pagan acceptance of the advancing years. " It is man's duty," writes Marcus Aurelius, "to comfort himself and wait for natural dissolution and not to be vexed but to find refreshment solely in these thoughts—first that nothing will happen to me which is not conformable to the nature of the Universe."[1] How melancholy the tone of this noble utterance, to which we must return later in the book.

Now, the religious man of any faith, basing his life on a very different theory, is bound by the same laws of nature but cannot share the sadness of the pagan Emperor. He must wince at that odious expression that a man is past his prime. Given eternity, there is no prime. So crude a phrase is proper to the butcher shop or cattle market and wholly inept when used about the soul. The religious man respects the courage of the pagan but must reject his theory, for he cannot persuade himself that it squares with the facts of life. The following pages make no other point than this.

Yet life is not so easy for the religious man. In theory he is clear in his mind about the life beyond this one but in practice he hesitates. Indeed unless he is very careful he will fall between this world and the next.

Compelled, as he is, to live and work among men who accept no other life than this one, he may without intention adopt a semi-pagan attitude to middle age. He will develop double vision, experiencing both the disillusionment of pagans and the threatening shadow of the deity ahead. Death seems a double agony, for the undertaker, sombre and black hatted, is a sign both of the beginning and the end. Double vision leads to a double verdict on himself. This life is for him the only real life and yet he must spoil it with a sense of guilt and fear about the next. As he gets older he is a aware that he is past his prime and good for nothing, yet his wretched soul goes marching on. Great unhappiness is tasted by religious people through such an inconsistency. Any effort is worthwhile to force oneself to see middle age in true perspective and to base one's life on solid fact. Better, in a sense, the straightforward pagan approach than this effort to serve two masters which leaves one with the worst of two worlds.

The full implications of middle age, all the glorious opportunities which its years can release for us, cannot be grasped in a second or set out in simple sentences covering a page or two. You must be patient with yourself and with the author in his double and possibly unrewarding effort to carry coals to Newcastle while teaching his grandmother to suck eggs. Here, at the very start, as remote preparation for that self-knowledge which is so essential, it may help to set out three fundamental changes which are likely to occur in middle age. If we note, too, how these changes interact, we come to appreciate how problems which we have isolated in separate compartments are no more than different aspects of the same phase of development. Just as puberty was not confined to glands but affected our whole attitude to the world about us, so changes in middle age may have many side effects.

THE THREE PRESSURES

The most obvious of these changes will occur in our physical condition which is for ever balancing and adjusting itself to the shifting pace of life. Thus, babies have their own peculiar problems, irritations, tendencies and habits and harried mothers are buttressed by the promise that the little ones will grow out of them one fine day. They do, but only to pass to the boils and Brylcreem of the teen-age world. The same pattern of physical change continues after adolescence and we may expect similar bodily alterations throughout middle age. The great climacteric, a subject of enormous concern to our grandparents, seems to have yielded to modern medicine and to have lost many of its terrors today. Nevertheless, both for women and for men, the sexual changes in maturity may still produce psychological and spiritual effects. Other alterations in the body, in circulation, digestive capacity, nervous energy may demand radical adjustments in our way of prayer. Who knows for example all the causes and complications when, in middle age, we suddenly put on weight? Legs are thrown off balance by this added tonnage and the poor old toes, in coping with an unexpected burden, alter their grip and so develop corns. Now corns, though relatively unimportant in the ascent to heaven, may yet play havoc on certain days with our spiritual life. Or, again, I have seen a confident, outward-looking man develop scruples after a simple operation for hernia.

B

Worry about coughing in his case led to worry about everything else. Anyone of us who has tried to slim will know how any tampering with the diet can cause mental and spiritual distress. Even a change of eyesight, restricting, as it may, our powers of observation, will tend to make us think too much about ourselves.

This point of physical change and its effect on the soul would seem almost too obvious to mention, were it not the fact that an astonishing number of people are unwilling to make any allowance in their own case. I have seen sensible men and women worrying themselves sick because, at fifty, they cannot sleep as soundly as they did at ten. Insomnia brings with it panic about impure thoughts. Panic means sleeping pills and the last state of that sufferer is worse than the first. Others fret as though their memory was failing because they cannot now carry telephone numbers and Christian names. They take no acccount of the fact that, when younger, they had far less to remember, whereas now, their memory, like their boxroom, is crammed with the assorted rubbish of forty years.

This is no medical treatise; details of physical change may be studied elsewhere and here we are concerned with one fact only, that our bodily condition must be considered in questions of prayer. Physical change does not necessarily imply deterioration and though there is bound to be a gradual running down of certain faculties, compensations should be noted too. The following summary of expected change, made by a doctor, underlines this. Dr George Lawton writes: "Physically you do not change as much from thirty to forty as you did between twenty-five and thirty; from fifty to seventy-five as from forty to fifty-five. Your eyes began to age at ten, your hearing at about twenty. By thirty your muscular strength, reaction time and reproductive powers have reached their peak. On the other hand your mind is still young and growing at fifty; your brain does not reach its zenith until ten years after that. From sixty on, mental efficiency declines very slowly to the age of eighty."[2]

It is reassuring to note that we need not become more stupid and that our mental capacity increases year by year. In this it comes second to our spiritual evolution, which continues until the end of our lives. Whatever may be happening to the other sections of the body, these two vital faculties expand. Few take advantage of this fact. Fewer still consider for a moment the importance of adjusting their behaviour to exercise the two qualities which are best able to cope with middle age. For the rest, we would make a mistake if we imagined that we must necessarily suffer more in middle age. One need only teach in a preparatory school, as I have done, to see with amazement how much pain and sickness is borne by little boys and girls. Many of us will suffer far less in middle age than we did when we were young. The greatest single trouble at our stage in life is worry, and here children may look down on us pityingly.

The mention of worry leads us to the second fundamental change of middle age. Nerves, as we call them, produce a crop of problems harder to diagnose and far more difficult to cure. A general practitioner has the easier task as he checks our blood pressure, prescribes pills to correct our deficiencies, alters our diet to give our legs and toes a chance. The psychiatrist will also try to help but he is too often dealing with people who are not prepared to admit to nervous strain. Statistics vary but there is, today, well nigh universal agreement that more than half the diseases of middle age are mentally induced. One honest G.P., discussing his surgery experience with me, reckoned that 90% of his patients needed the help of a psychiatrist.

The psychological changes in middle age are of profound importance because our happiness here and hereafter may possibly turn on the way in which we handle them. I have seen patients dying of cancer who were happy, but one cannot find a happy patient among those who are nursing a grouse. Scruples, bees in the bonnet, sexual aberrations, chronic depression, drain all the joy from life. They spill over from the mind to affect the body and also debilitate the soul. Worse still, they ruin other people's lives as well. Self-pity, for example, not only hurts the patient but leaves a train of misery in its wake. The neurotic sickness of parents will not end on their own deathbed but will be perpetuated in their children's attitude to life. How frequently one meets scrupulous, anxious, unhappy people who owe their misery to the example set when they were young!

Many of our mental disturbances are progressive, spreading from one sphere of life to another until life itself is unbearable. When the jury returns a verdict of "unsound mind" it is rather too late to go back to the causes, to that moment in early middle age when they might have been cured.

Today, everyone is alert to physical threats and symptoms and the TV advertisements love to show us the germs gnawing at our bodies before they are routed by the very latest cure. We have innumerable lotions

and sprays to cope with catarrh or dandruff but how
rarely one sees an advertisement for psychiatry. Can it
be that the sale of drugs would fall too swiftly if the
causes of mental worry were solved successfully? A
great deal of this book will be devoted to these psychological troubles which may be cured only by a philosophy of life. Almost every chapter will deal with their
mastery or alleviation, for so many of them are spiritual
in cause. Mental distress and tension is common in
middle age because of the duplicity and conflict which
all egocentric people experience. Frustrated ambition
plays an important part in much mental illness and
here pyschology leads us to the spiritual.

The third fundamental change in middle age is
spiritual. Oddly enough, we never seem to expect such
a change or to be ready for it, nor are we alert enough
to recognize its signs. We may see the change in others
or study it in biographies without ever troubling to
apply it to ourselves. Somehow we never grasp that the
physical and psychological alterations which are going
on within us may play a vital part in the development
of the soul. Why, a prolonged or serious illness may be
one of the greatest spiritual experiences that a man can
have.

The psychological and the spiritual are so closely
connected that it is hard to know whether to consult a
psychiatrist or a priest. Modern pyschology has become
for many a substitute for religion, probing the depths
of human personality without seeking or accepting
evidence of man's spiritual roots. Earlier antagonism
between the Church and psychiatry has now given way
to tolerance. Christians would not now deny that many
symptoms, formerly classed as purely spiritual, may

now be accepted as signs of mental distress. So scruples, hallucinations, mystical experiences, sudden conversions, diabolic possession, while spiritual in content, may be psychological in cause. On the other hand, many distinguished psychiatrists have been men of deep religious principle. These would readily accept a spiritual world and a type of problem which will never be solved on the psychiatrist's couch. I have seen many who have been much helped by psychiatry but no lasting cure has been possible because what the patient really needed was a Christian attitude to life. How much of our modern tension comes from this spiritual emptiness. It is painfully hard to face middle age and what lies beyond it when life itself seems to lack any point.

It was once very fashionable to explain all spiritual experience in terms of pyschology but, as always, the extremists carried it too far. Medical materialism— William James's phrase—no longer satisfies with its glib assertion that Paul outside Damascus suffered a lesion of the occipital cortex, that Teresa of Avila was an hysteric and Francis of Assisi an hereditary degenerate. Undoubtedly conversion in middle age is one of the most baffling and radical of spiritual changes and no medical jargon will cover or explain the subtleties of each individual case. Nor need we fall back on the evidence of emotional women, for five of the most famous accounts of sudden conversions, three ancient and two modern, were written by hard-headed men. In our own day Douglas Hyde, the Communist news editor, and Group Captain Leonard Cheshire, V.C.,[3] the war ace, have set out in detail the cause and sequence of their change. A century ago Newman, the Oxford don, told the same story, as did Ignatius of Loyola, the sixteenth-century soldier, and Augustine, the fifth-century African philosopher. St Ignatius of Loyola not only experienced such a change himself but he devised a method by which thousands of men and women of every type and in every country might experience the same. Those who know the spiritual exercises of St Ignatius, not in theory but in practice, will have no doubt about the reality of such a spiritual change.

I mention these celebrated accounts of spiritual conversion not only as an example of fundamental spiritual change in mature people but, further, as an encouragement. We, too, may well have to change. Spiritual adjustment in middle age is often necessary and far more frequent than most of us would ever guess. William James wrote with so much sensitiveness of these conversions which, psychologically, are extreme enough to be called a new birth. Men who have lived as agnostics for many years suddenly turn religious and, in the case of Augustine and Ignatius, end up as saints. It is astonishing the number of saints who experienced a conversion of some sort. Sinners, too, may qualify. Thousands who have long abandoned all religious practice suddenly find themselves restless for want of faith. How many priests have had the gratifying experience of instructing those who seek religion with minds which are theologically a blank. Nor should we dodge the opposite form of conversion when those who have faithfully practised religion from early childhood suddenly and painfully abandon it in middle age. In these two cases we may see the more extreme form of religious change.

Spiritual alterations in middle age must not, however, be restricted to these sudden conversions as though here was our chief and only goal. All manner of subtle changes may be noted in man's mature approach to God. Some people move smoothly forward without trouble while others come up against a barrier of doubts. Not a few feel that they are losing their faith and, while they continue from habit to perform their religious exercises, they judge themselves hypocrites. Fear, which was not present in childhood and adolescence, often enters religion in middle age. It comes with the vivid realization of death. Another peculiar symptom is the guilt complex which distorts religion and focuses attention exclusively on sin. Bunyan in *Pilgrim's Progress* outlines the spiritual trials of many religious people, the worst of which is the slough of despond. There are more cheerful changes, too, and far more people than most of us would imagine become increasingly aware of the presence of God. Prayer changes for them from thoughts, words and actions into a quiet recollection of God. Mystical experiences are not uncommon with the fear and uncertainty which these often bring. I knew a priest who deliberately struggled against such mystical inclinations for fear of pride and of deluding himself. Most common of all in middle age is a deep sense of failure among those who attained to a high standard in their youth. They are thrown out of their stride by sexual thoughts and desires which they could always master twenty years ago. They could pray then, now they cannot pray. They used to go to Mass daily, now they just about manage once a week. Are they, in fact, careless or is this the typical middle-aged quirk of self-reproach?

If physical and mental states may be eased by adjustment, spiritual problems will also respond to a more mature approach. Would it be too audacious to suggest on this most vital of all our undertakings, that one can take oneself and one's salvation too seriously? Childish anxiety is no virtue even in the spiritual sphere. Fretting achieves so little and merely discloses a pusillanimous approach to God. Yet fretting is surprisingly common; the timid steward of the parable, who tied his talent in a napkin, seems to have many descendants, male and female, alive today.

If, and rightly, we tease the man who thinks that he is senile every time he forgets a telephone number, should we not also laugh at ourselves when we judge ourselves slack, adulterous or damned? How few of us are prepared to laugh at our crazy moods. That much of our worry is dishonest may be proved in a minute, stemming as it does from culpable ignorance. We are not prepared to find out the truth about God. We, who have reached middle age well abreast of so many secular subjects, still have a fifth-form mentality in our spiritual life.

Years of experience, with myself, first, and then with others, have led me to the conclusion that we are, most of us, mentally retarded in all that concerns God. More than half of our troubles in middle age: scruples, slackness, fear, melancholy, moods and panics, arise from ignorance of our own machinery and laziness in thinking and reading about God. Our knowledge of God, of the Scriptures, of sin, our understanding of the Church and of religion have not increased in forty years. Our religious outlook is childish, far below the level of our capacity. Mature men and women, who read widely and deeply on other subjects, draw the line at an occasional pamphlet about spiritual things. Spiritually we have moved no further than the *Water Babies* and *Hereward the Wake*. Before worrying about loss of faith, we should examine our library lists. "Look your age," drawls every U.S. Marshal to each maladjusted cowboy and such homely counsel might well apply to most of us in middle age.

Others are not to blame for our personal negligence in this matter but some have played a part in holding us back. A misgotten prejudice seeks to retard religious maturity by extolling the simple faith of children, peasants, Irish grannies and youthful saints. Lip-service is paid to Aquinas but I have yet to hear a preacher who suggested that we, in our limited way, might copy him. Spiritual writers and directors so easily turn paternal, extolling the virtue of obedience as though it were an alternative to thinking for ourselves. Child-like obedience on essential doctrines is a glorious virtue but it becomes merely childish when extended to those fringe devotions not of the deposit of faith. That a saint popularized such a devotion, that it has helped thousands, should draw from me not unthinking acceptance but due respect. Looking back from middle age to those happy days when we piled saint on saint and nine holy Mondays onto ten holy Tuesdays, we come to judge our present state too harshly, confusing slackness with maturity. Someone said to me recently, "My faith has gone to pot; I used to say the rosary daily when I was younger, now I'm lucky if I get through one Our Father and that half asleep."

Far be it from me to advocate semi-somnolence in prayer or the abandonment of any devotions; in the middle fifties I find myself resuming many of them again. They have their place in the spiritual life but they are not essential; to try to gauge one's progress by them may be to retard maturity. So busy have we been, worrying about devotional practice, that we have barely read the Gospel, never St Paul. The works of Augustine, Teresa of Avila, Francis de Sales are unknown to us; small wonder we have so many fears, panics, doubts. So many of these very doubts are doubts about childish concepts which we should have discarded years ago. An intelligent woman, troubled with doubts, at length had to admit that she had lost her faith in angels and this because she could no longer swallow the feathers in their wings. This may sound ridiculous but it happens to be true. Any number of middle-aged people find their faith less robust. Few are prepared to search for the causes for fear of disloyalty. Rather than read and think for themselves, they fill up the gaps with an amalgam of popular devotions, never grasping that their souls are undernourished, are, in fact, starving for God.

Is it too late to start in middle age? The slick reply would be "better late than never" but words like "late" and "never" have little meaning when set against eternity. In this new and exciting spiritual world in which the last shall be first and the first last; in which full pay is given at the eleventh hour, now is the time to begin.

It is just possible that most of us could not have started our search for God before this moment, for it is only in middle age that we grasp the urgency. All our past years have been working towards this point. They were not wasted for they have brought us to our present maturity. Some of us may have rejected previous opportunities but not all. Take my own case. Six times

in my life I have read the *Confessions of St Augustine*
and yet only now, in the middle fifties, do I begin to
comprehend the message which he seeks to convey. The
words, the thoughts, the plan of the book have not
altered throughout the centuries; I read the same
sentences now that I read thirty years ago. The change
is not in Augustine but in myself. The cold fact is that
one begins to take religion seriously only when one
is vividly aware of death. Where, in youth, death was
a macabre threat to other and older people, it suddenly
becomes in middle age a definite entry on one's engagement pad. William James could write that sanctity
comes with the recognition of the crisis of the present
moment—the young saints saw it and died sooner; we
old lags meet reality only in middle age.

IMPORTANCE OF SELF-KNOWLEDGE
AS A MEANS TO AN END

If you ask me how one should begin to face religious
reality, I can but reply that self-knowledge is the
one and only way. The whole of this first chapter has
been moving towards this. I will never conquer fear,
never pray with ease, never enjoy life or attain self-
fulfilment until I am familiar with my own spiritual
machinery. The other chapters of this book may expand this theme and provide a comment if here, at the
very beginning, we accept the need.

The Greeks recognized this need and, over the
entrance to Apollo's temple in ancient Delphi, they
placed the inscription "Know thyself". For the modern
pilgrim, too, such a warning is essential; we must begin
here and nowhere else. Why? It is the mark of a genuine

craftsman to know the tools which he is going to use. On the golf course, in the concert hall, at the factory bench, round the racing circuit, the genius of the great performer lies in his handling of his instruments. In motor racing, a second's hesitation may cost one the trophy, in show jumping. the rider wins who best adapts himself to the moods and vagaries of his mount. Or, put the lesson the other way round. Have you suffered the misfortune of sitting in a car next to an indifferent driver who muffs the gears and maltreats the clutch? Yes, the car moves along but out of harmony and under protest with the engine revving and the wrong indicator blinking a caustic commentary. The driver may curse the makers, the cops, the traffic lights, his fellow drivers; he hardly knows his own stupidity well enough to curse himself.

Few people really know themselves. We live in a fool's paradise, ignorant even of our manner and appearance though one might have thought that these were easy enough to check. A recording machine gives a very different impression of our voice and accent while a tailor's cunning mirror provides a less flattering view of the back of the neck. We cannot even look ourselves in the face. Writes Rudolf Allers:

> We have to look into a mirror for the sake of discovering what our face is like. But we never see, unless we make use of a special arrangement, our face as it is and as others see it because the mirror shows on the right side what, in fact, is on the left side and vice versa. Nobody's face is so symmetrical that it remains unaltered by exchanging its halves. This is, for that matter, the reason why most people feel dissatisfied by pictures which have been taken of them even when others declare

these pictures to be perfect as to likeness. No one is used to seeing himself as the lens pictures him.[4]

If we are wrong about our looks, how honest is our assessment of our day-to-day behaviour, of our humour, our tolerance or our truthfulness? How easily we dismiss the comments of others, spoken in good faith. A man pooh-poohs the idea that he works too hard, smokes too much, is restless, irritable, impatient, though his wife and children and friends all agree on the point. Can he truly believe that they are all wrong? Yes, he can, so false is his opinion of himself. As Aldous Huxley puts it:

> Ignorance of self is something that answers to this description. In its origins it is voluntary, for by introspection and by listening to other people's judgments of our character, we can, if we so desire, come to a shrewd understanding of our flaws and weaknesses and the real, as opposed to the avowed and advertised motives of our actions. If most of us remain ignorant of ourselves, it is because self-knowledge is painful and we prefer the pleasure of illusion . . . without self-knowledge there can be no true humility, therefore no effective self-naughting, therefore no unitive knowledge of the divine Ground underlying the self and ordinarily eclipsed by it.[5]

Do not be discouraged; "Know thyself" implies a great deal more than "Know thy faults". It must include as well a working knowledge of our virtues, and these, too, are often hidden from our eyes. At heart most people are pathetically humble, well-intentioned and generous. They form an unflattering picture of themselves because their vision is shrouded by a haze of superficial defects. A man's very brashness is face-saving, more for the sake of his wife and children than from any conceit in himself. The holier the persons, the lower their opinion of themselves. How often I have wished, when, after a funeral, the mourners gather for refreshments, that the deceased could pop in for a few minutes to hear those very virtues praised in him which he had known for certain that he lacked.

Know thyself. It is natural, I suppose that self-knowledge should start with our own moral behaviour, for here is a practical field over which we may exercise some control. Self-knowledge must never end with this. Almost all those who have heard of the book, jump to the wrong conclusion that St Augustine in his *Confessions* is writing about his previous, wicked life.[6] The great African doctor mentions his past weaknesses and is duly contrite but two-thirds of his book is concerned with a confession, not of his sins, but of the glory and mercy of God. Augustine devotes several chapters to the use of the memory and this will surprise us until we grasp that only a knowledge of how our memory works will enable us to use the memory to find God. St Teresa of Avila shows us the importance of self-knowledge when she tells us that we can never know ourselves unless we are seeking to know God. Much harm is done by those who identify self-knowledge with self-examination; in this book, at least, it implies a working knowledge of all our gears and flaps and levers that softly and smoothly we may leave the ground.

It is, as I have said, often or only in middle age that we come to appreciate self-knowledge and to seek to acquire it. We discover with shame how little we know of ourselves. We see, at last, that such ignorance has led to present frustration and to past mistakes. We

have never studied the powers of our soul, the relationship between reason and emotion, the dangers of a
faulty imagination, the full implications of the various
levels of the soul. Some people know so little of themselves that they spend half their lives cultivating in-
dividualism as a typically English virtue, never guessing
the misery that this will bring to them in the days ahead.
Others, from a wrong sense of virtue, exclude from their
lives those glorious emotions which would have led
them speedily to God. How many glorious and loving
people through a wrong notion have assumed a harsh,
puritan mentality? Unless we know ourselves we will
start examining our consciences for the wrong symptoms and end by confessing the wrong sins. An inaccurate picture of God may mean the wrong type of
prayer, fruitless striving after phoney virtue in imitation of an imaginary Christ who is sheer caricature.

How then set out to know ourselves? Each must
decide his own form of examination, the method
which will suit him best. Sitting in a favourite chair,
lying in bed, pacing the moors, driving a car down
unfrequented by-ways, one must snatch the apt occasion to talk to oneself. Some of us may have been doing
this for years, others are shy of introspection, switch-
ing on the radio to drown inconvenient thoughts.

My whimsy would suggest an interview in a bedroom or bathroom, around us the symbols of our
earthly state. In most bathrooms there is one cupboard choked with beauty preparations, pre-shave
lotions, lipstick, scissors, tweezers, all the gimmicks
that we must rely on before we face the world of men.
In another cupboard are sleeping pills, gargle, aspirin,
antiseptics to remind us of the ceaseless, weary battle

which we all must lose in the end. Between the cup-
boards is the mirror showing our right ear on the left
side of our head.

There are holier places than a bathroom but few
more expressive; why, the only other piece of furniture
like a bath is a coffin: a bath with handles instead of
taps and a brass plate on the lid. Talk to God in the bath
and your prayer will be free of humbug, ask him and
he will certainly help you to know yourself.

2

UPWARDS, DOWNWARDS, SIDEWAYS

THE search for self-knowledge demands much patience, and disaster faces those who rush ahead. The pilgrim need never lack advice or directions, for an impressive number of great spiritual writers have described the journey, step by step. Each must choose among the experts for himself. Language presents a special problem, for in writing of the spirit each author must grope for words, metaphors, expressions to convey an experience peculiar to himself.

St Teresa of Avila saw the soul "as a castle made of a single diamond or a very clear crystal in which there are many rooms".[1] St Augustine chose a similar explanation as he found himself mounting "through the fields and vast palaces of memory, a spreading, limitless room within myself". St John of the Cross and St Francis de Sales also describe the journey upwards but with less emphasis on rooms.

St Catherine of Siena, on the other hand, finds herself working downwards until she discovers her real self inhabiting an inner cell. A modern writer, Dom Bede Griffiths, also refers to an inner sanctuary. Frequent references to the depths of the soul by many writers seem to imply descent. Yet Eckhart takes a very different image and sees the soul as wrapt in "thirty or forty hides like an ox or a bear". St Teresa, never short of ideas or afraid to mix them, leaves her Interior Castle to call our attention to the Spanish *palmito*. She compares our soul to this fruit from which all the prickly leaves must be taken before the delicious kernel is disclosed. Whatever the metaphors used, all the authors are seeking to warn us that we must uncover ourselves by stages and that the process may take time. One modern writer, Dr Sherwood Taylor, well-known author of chemistry text-books, sees us as living on three different levels simultaneously, a view which appeals very much to me. Dr Sherwood Taylor[2] keeps very close to St Francis de Sales.[3]

OUR LIFE IN PUBLIC

Following his plan, we start with our life in public, our 'real' life as most young people would call it, based on the senses and centred on the world of men. Whether we, later, see ourselves as climbing upwards, downwards or sideways, at least we all started life on ground level and in a pram. We reacted instinctively to the world about us, especially to milk. Life for us was life in the world of people and, with a vocabulary short and incoherent, we made contact by means of chuckles, screams and tears.

No need to delay unduly though it is instructive and rewarding to turn to the memories of those distant days. Experts assert with good reason that the lessons, habits, tendencies acquired in early childhood have fashioned our pattern of behaviour throughout the years. At the age of three, we began to form simple judgments, compiling our short list of enemies and friends. We also began to adapt means to an end. However, in the main, we surrendered to our senses, experiencing life without much conscious thought.

As to God in our infant years, he seemed as real as any other character in the story books. We pictured him as a superman and followed the conventional illustrations of the artists who drew him thus. For most of us, he was powerful, well intentioned, kindly but very angry if we told a lie. Our parents seemed to know him well and he was, definitely, on their side. Had we suddenly been informed that he did not exist at all, that our parents had made him up with Father Christmas, we might have mourned him for a week.

More important than these childish memories are the three unconscious pressures which played so powerful a part in our youthful development. The first is imitation, a quality not often heeded but very strong in childhood and active in us even now. The desire to be a man, to be a man like Daddy, remains a powerful influence throughout life. Animals imitate easily but no parrot with its string of second-hand obscenities can challenge the imitative instinct of a man. Far more than any animal, men imitate each other, a worrying fact which all parents and teachers have to bear in mind. Some of us in middle age still derive a childish pleasure from performing those acts, acquiring the status symbols which we so much admired in our formative years. The thrill of long trousers still survives, the pride in dressing for dinner, in offering drinks and dispensing tips. Nor can we resist the temptation to talk like a Dutch uncle from time to time. To see some hoary old warrior with a new gadget is to recognize that the child is father to the man.

Unconscious imitation explains so many an old and odd tradition in our lives. Class mannerisms stem from this and local dialects. political loyalties. school customs, regimental lore and undergraduate dress. Thus, too, prejudice is born, strong enough to last a lifetime and bitter enough to poison a million human relationships. The power of the TV screen derives from this tendency towards imitation; its impact will be fully gauged only when those who have been reared on it from childhood reach middle age.

Imitation is the first, unconscious influence in life which leads us to the second; quite early in our lives we begin to act. Wrote one devil to another in the glorious *Screwtape Letters*, "All mortals tend to turn into the thing that they are pretending to be".

We are all actors in our public lives. The fact deserves attention, for self-knowledge turns on it. When Shakespeare wrote "All the world's a stage" he described just this. We each play many parts. The silly little girl who lisps and rolls her eyes is a budding actress, differing only in age from her beloved mother whose face is thick with paint. Superficially, women are worse than men in this. Like actresses they make-up their faces every day. Lipstick, foundation cream, nail enamel, hair dye, eyebrow tweezers are the tools of one who hopes very much to be seen.

Men may feel superior but they, too, are actors with clothes and uniforms hired from Moss Bros. or supplied by the Establishment. The barrister's wig, the major's moustache, the parson's collar are props. Social life is theatrical on any level; the left-wing intellectual, the sturdy Trades Union leader, the shop steward, as often as not is unconsciously acting the part. Put any human being within striking distance of another and both seek ways and means of 'putting themselves across'. We have our parts, the glamour girl, the devoted mother, the cynic, the old soldier, the melancholy Jaques. Given the same situation, we dutifully pull the same grimaces, assume the same postures, crack the same jokes. By middle age we know all our scripts by heart. A playwright has only to copy our antics exactly to have the audience in fits of laughter and whispering to each other, "How very true to life". Augustine made a caustic comment on this sham. He writes: "I was preparing an oration in honour of the Emperor in which I was to utter any number of lies to win the applause of people who knew that they were lies".

How about God and religion in our public lives? The point will be treated more fully later, here we need do no more than note the fact. As with all our other activities, religion on this public level is played upon a stage. This does not make it wrong—indeed the liturgy could hardly be other than theatrical—for religion must fit itself to the way in which men are made. We kneel, we stand, we sing in chorus, we robe ourselves in vestments, for these are the natural gestures by which we express ourselves. Religious acting on this public level is not optional but essential, because we are men. Sufficient to note that it is none too difficult to turn it into humbug as the Pharisees have proved. The very word 'humbug' leads us to look towards the second level of life where is decided the type of part that we will play upon life's stage.

Sitting in a favourite chair, lying in bed, tramping the moors or singing in the bathroom, we should draw from our own experience examples of the way in which we act. No blame is here attached. We simply want to note the way in which our life has developed since the day when we stepped down from the pram.

From imitation of our elders, how easily we passed to acting to impress our parents, masters, boy friend, girl friend, employer, colleagues, enemies and friends. Most of us discover in middle age that it is less and less easy to impress those who know us well. Our wives and children know our act by heart. Here lies one of the most serious obstacles to happy marriage and a fact which explains why it is that a man who is charming and gay with strangers turns sad and broody as he fits his key to his own front door. Artificial love, the stage row, the comic patter have small success at home. How many marriages fall to pieces because they were part social, part theatrical, part imitation and cannot survive without an audience. Sometimes we use the expression "she saw through him", a powerful description of an act that has failed.

When we 'see through' a person, a scene, a situation, we move from the public world of men and women to the higher level of life on which we live. Parallel with our life in public is our life in private, the life of an actor who has left the stage for his dressing-room. We are alone in our rooms. In one sense we are more ourselves when no one is watching, when the bedroom door or bathroom door, like a stage curtain, cuts us off from the audience. We let our hair down, put our feet up, shed our manners with our other props. What price table manners, a loving smile, an Oxford accent when one is without an audience?

OUR LIFE IN PRIVATE

We are more ourselves in our rooms, more relaxed, more honest, more humble, more critical. We may hum a snatch or two, dance about the room, play a game with the nail brush, challenge ourselves to a competition, try to wind the bath plug round the hot tap using only our toes. Often enough we begin and end with the mirror, studying each wrinkle, patting our hair, searching anxiously for any symptoms of cancer of the tongue. Most of us have an unexplained lump in our bodies which might get bigger and certainly must be watched. Augustine, again, makes a shrewd observation : "We are not much given to laughter when we are alone".

This private life of ours may prove bewildering, even painful, and many seek to avoid it if they can. They dread to be 'shut in'. Some are frightened of their own company, others bored. This fear of ourselves deserves analysis for it is powerful enough at times to throw us into panic and its victims will go to any lengths to distract their minds. They write pointless and unnecessary letters or stare vacantly at Television in a desperate effort to find some kind of audience. I have known a woman who spent three hours daily on the phone. For some there is the endless hunt for bigger and better thrillers which they will read, propped up with pillows, until the last split second before their weary eyelids close. To dodge the same fear, an increasing number bolster their courage with drink. For others sexual thoughts provide the only distraction strong enough to offer an escape. Without an audience, so many are thrown off balance, they must talk at all costs to the cat or the canary or, if playing patience, to the Queen of Hearts. Religiously-minded folk rely on pious statues and chat to the holy ones that these represent.

It would be wrong to omit the point that while the

majority shun solitude, a minority seek it and find self-fufilment there. A recluse is often a coward, preferring loneliness to failure before an audience. On the other hand, some of the gayest and most successful freely end their days in hermitages or behind high convent walls. St Teresa of Avila is their spokesman, one of the liveliest of women who ever wrote a book.

Our private lives will lead us to a further stage if we have the courage, but for many it remains unfruitful. no more than an interlude before they step onto the stage again. These in their rooms attempt no more than a post-mortem on their past performance or a brief rehearsal for the next. They deliberately shut out any further introspection, preferring to describe themselves as 'down to earth'. To occupy their minds, they surrender to the third and strongest pressure which, in one form or another, assails us all.

We have already considered how our lives began with unconcious imitation and then moved to acting before our fellow men. Imagination, next, takes a hand like a film camera, photographing each performance and then, as it were, playing it back to us on a screen inside our heads. We moon. We sit back and re-live each moment, blushing at our errors, applauding our success. We imagine ourselves in heroic situations, the darlings of a thousand glamorous and romantic tales. In private we share the dreams of Walter Mitty, but where a few see through the humbug, many allow themselves to be carried away. This idealization of self in a self-created world may become a full-time occupation, pleasant because as author-actor each can write the type of part which he would like to play. More will be said of this weakness in a later chapter but it is well to note at this stage in our progress the harm that such a habit may play in our private lives.

How about God in our private lives? How about religion? It is in our bathrooms and our bedrooms that we come to the parting of the ways. If we refuse to go further in our quest for self-knowledge, then, by a devious path, we return to earth again. God will then be for us a filmed image of the superman of our baby days. I say 'filmed' because his image will lack precision but he will retain the features and postures assigned to him by the artists who illustrate children's books. Yes, we love him very much but, then, we created him. We may in private go through the gestures of prayer and worship because we derive a certain satisfaction for ourselves. We take it for granted that he loves us and has our interests at heart. As these interests are down-to-earth, he must come down to earth as well. He becomes the patient recipient of many earnest prayers for family, money, reputation, holidays, fine weather and good health.

It is not uncommon to meet those who, in their lives, have experienced many spiritual favours and can claim to have had those sudden flashes of union and intuition about which they have read in the lives of the saints. Self-idealization is not uncommon even in spiritual affairs. Some, at one stage or another, have undergone a type of sudden conversion, the memory of which survives to charm their private life for years. The devils in the *Screwtape Letters* knew all about such conversions and could cope with them. Unless a man is prepared to go forward to true self-knowledge, such ephemeral, spiritual experiences may do positive harm. They carry with them the slight phosphorescent glow

of an incipient halo and persuade the wearer that he
has the ear of God. In the parable of the sower a plant
was described which was all leaves and no fruit.

The ascent becomes more stiff as we mount to the
third level of our existence and it may help to survey
the general situation before entering it ourselves.

Even those who elect to go no further are certainly
aware of this inner life. The clues are too obvious and
the urge to follow them too pressing to be disregarded
even by those who are bad at heights. In our earliest
years when we were preoccupied with the exciting
world outside us, we were yet aware of this fuller
form of life inside ourselves. Children hear the inner
voice of conscience and know of a conflict in themselves. As we get older, this interior situation becomes
much more clear. Thus, we seem to have two wills.
Augustine in one of his most famous passages asks why
it is that if I command my arm and leg, both obey immediately, while if I tell myself to do some task, I fail
to obey myself. We have two wills, we have second
thoughts and are certainly double-faced. In earlier
times men saw this conflict as a battle between soul and
body, the one spiritual and exalted, the other carnal
and dragging the spirit down. Such a simple solution
now seems less satisfactory for the conflict is in the
soul itself. Shakespeare displays his genius most fully in
the dramatic presentation of this conflict inside a man.
You and I may not speak such exalted language but
we, too, soliloquize in the bathroom with less art but
as much pain as Hamlet or Macbeth.

Language, which was devised by men to meet concrete situations, expresses both the inner conflict and
our duplicity. Many everyday phrases reveal the other

Me inside us as when we say, "He fairly gave himself away". Again I might say, "I can read his thoughts" or "I can see through him", both suggesting a difference between himself on the surface and himself deep down inside. Two distinct people seem to be supposed in such phrases as "She so far forgot herself"; "She was beside herself with anger"; "Pull yourself together"; "Oh she is wrapped up in herself". Such language matches our experience on many occasions when we talk to ourselves. We seem to be two persons in one and the endless conversation between us is the one constant feature in all human life.

Schizophrenia is a mental sickness, better known as split personality, but even the sanest of us is born with a potential crack. Jung, in the last of his books, not yet published in England, makes clear the position thus: "The play and counterplay between personalities One and Two which has run through my whole life, has nothing to do with a 'split' or dissociation in the ordinary medical sense. On the contrary it is played out in every individual." Or take the excellent description by Alphonse Daudet, quoted by William James: "This horrible duality has often given me matter for reflection. Oh this terrible second Me, always seated while the other is on foot, acting, living, suffering, bestirring itself. This second Me that I have never been able to intoxicate, to make shed tears, to put to sleep. And how it sees into things and how it mocks."[4]

Yes, this second Me is within us whether we care for the idea or not. Sufficient for us to accept the fact and to grasp that there is a higher level of life, shared with no others and, hence, very much harder to delineate. No library could hold all the books written on so profound a subject towards which so many sciences converge. Endless research on a variety of aspects may have solved the fringe problems but the central experience is too individual to be explained by anyone but our individual selves.

The very size of the investigations into man's inner composition must frighten most amateurs away. Thus, Augustine was preoccupied with the wonders of the memory, a power which seems wider than the soul who owns it, seeing that I may sit back and remember myself. William James, Jung and the other great psychologists probe the significance of behaviour patterns, the force of habit, the weird influence of the unconscious, the complexes and tensions of the divided self. Meantime, Freud was studying the significance of sex, not only of the appetite, about which we read so much on the physical level, but of the far more profound reactions to sex deep within ourselves.

When the Greeks hoisted the inscription "Know thyself" over the temple at Delphi, they were setting themselves and us a task which may only partly be fulfilled. Doctors and psychologists work on but one small section of the human machinery while philosophers and theologians are engaged in a wider and far more abstract field. Take Cardinal Newman's precise paragraph about our modes of thought. He sums up man's intellectual activity thus: "It is the characteristic of our minds to be ever engaged in passing judgment on the things that come before us; no sooner do we apprehend than we judge; we allow nothing to stand by itself, we compare, contrast, abstract, generalize, connect, adjust, classify."[5]

While Newman is doing all this, Teresa of Avila and

John of the Cross, to mention two great friends out of
hundreds of mystical writers, are compiling books on
that mysterious, higher part of the human soul. It is
fascinating to follow them there. They seem to speak a
different language to meet a situation which many
have experienced but which is almost too personal to
explain.

There are, too, the poets whose twofold genius
enables them to penetrate by intuition into the very
marrow of our being and to express their vision in
lovely language to delight us all. If we want to see in
a flash the long path leading to self-knowledge, we
should re-read the sonnet by Sassoon.

> "When I'm alone"—the words tripped off his tongue
> As though to be alone were nothing strange.
> "When I was young," he said; "when I was young. . . ."
> I thought of age, and loneliness, and change.
> I thought how strange we grow when we're alone,
> And how unlike the selves that meet and talk,
> And blow the candles out, and say good-night.
> Alone . . . the word is life endured and known.
> It is the stillness where our spirits walk
> And all but inmost faith is overthrown.[6]

We may not ourselves be able to write in this manner
but we know exactly what the poet is seeking to convey. The mystery of our inner life is always with us
and it is no surprise to me that so many are far too
frightened to march ahead. They prefer the dimensional
world with which they are familiar, the greeting of
neighbours, the bustle of the supermarket, the fun of
setting off in a car for the week-end. They fear that if
they think too much these simple pleasures may never
be quite the same again.

OUR LIFE IN THE CENTRE OF OUR HEARTS

Not all turn back. The realists are not those who choose what we call the real world, the world of three dimensions, but those who are curious enough and restless enough, even unhappy enough, to face the facts of life. They return right enough and though they come back different, their capacity for happiness is greater, never less. At the outset there are awkward moments and the frightening threat of loneliness. For our inner life cannot be shared. Even the parents who gave us our bodies can only guess what is going on inside our hearts and heads. The doctors and nurses who tend us in sickness, give us injections and arrange our pillows are rarely able to reach far enough inside us to comfort the sufferer beneath. Much of the dissatisfaction in confession stems from the fact that I cannot fully reveal my motives to the priest. Certain deep friendships afford some relief but, even in the intimacy of love-making, I may have secret, critical, even bitter thoughts about the one I profess to love. To quote Alphonse Daudet again in a passage which will strike a chord in most of us: "The first time that I perceived that I was two was at the death of my brother Henri, when my father cried out so dramatically, 'He is dead; he is dead'. While my first self wept, my second half thought, 'How well he declaimed that line; how fine it would sound in the theatre'. I was fourteen years old."

Certain difficulties face us when we try to describe this inner life. Because we are all so different, it is futile to generalize. Next, the subject is so vast that, from a mass of material, one has to pick and choose. Again, so many of the experts merely confuse us, their language is so technical and so baffling that ordinary untrained people despair of ever knowing themselves. Christ alone cuts right across the tangle of human language with a twelve-word sentence, only one word of which attains two syllables. He said to a critical audience, and there is a wealth of meaning in his simple sentence: "It is from the heart's overflow that the mouth speaks."

A deceptive simplicity shrouds the full meaning of these words. Carefully considered, they afford the perfect introduction to any study of our interior life. They offer an explanation of human behaviour and underline the motive which causes men to act as they do. Apply them to myself and I learn in a line that my behaviour, the words that I speak and the gestures with which I support them, the very figure that I cut or would like to cut in public, is determined by the sentiments formed in my heart. Christ tells us implicitly in this passage and explicitly on another similar occasion that good and evil are manufactured in the heart. They do not come fully fashioned from without. The senses are innocent when they pass their message to the brain. The brain itself, playing the part of a superior civil servant, performs its functions in the way described by Newman, comparing, contrasting, abstracting, adjusting, generalizing and then submitting its report. It is the heart that decides. The heart is King, President, Managing Director and its decisions pass to every department of my conscious life.

Clearly much turns on the meaning of the word 'heart'. This overworked substantive is employed in so many different senses that we must distinguish carefully between them if we are ever to reach the truth. Yet language is an admirable guide and we so often find incorporated in its delicate shades of meaning the subtle experiences which past generations knew and passed on to us.

Medically, the heart is but a lump of muscle, cunningly fashioned as a pump. Psychologically, the word covers a far wider area, in William James's phrase it stands for the centre of personal energy, "the hot, living point of consciousness". Language uses the word heart metaphorically in just this sense. If we say that a man has his heart in his job, we mean much more than that he completes the task and goes through the motions for we know that his whole, conscious enthusiasm has been engaged. A heart-to-heart talk differs from ordinary, trivial conversation in that the whole human person is committed to what he says. It is a giving of himself. We say that a man is broken-hearted when his girl jilts him where we could hardly say that he was broken-nosed or broken-legged. Nose and leg are part of his body but, happily, they do not share this emotional response. When language uses such vivid words as 'hard-hearted', lion-hearted', 'wholehearted', it is seeking to describe a deep, personal reaction, a reaction, moreover, which is somehow associated with the breast.

I read, years ago, and cannot now trace the reference, that the philosopher Spinoza maintained that his inner conversations took place in the region of his pancreas. Biological exactness is not here essential but many of us would support Spinoza's impression in this. We seem to talk to ourselves somewhere in our breasts.

The heart stands for a wholehearted commitment and there may be some medical support for this. The word 'heart' has been used throughout the centuries

D

because the physical heart seems to feel these personal responses, to suffer and rejoice in them. Is it for this reason that sudden, deep emotions may produce a heart attack?

"It is from the heart's overflow that the mouth speaks." Christ himself goes on to use the word heart in a whole series of simple lessons, each furthering and deepening the meaning of the original text. Thus, in the solemn setting of the Sermon on the Mount, he makes the important announcement: "Blessed are the clean of heart, for they shall see God". In contrast to this he remarked of the man who lusts after a woman that "he has already committed adultery with her in his heart". When the scribes were muttering against him, he asked them publicly, "Why do you cherish wicked thoughts in your hearts?" Elsewhere he accused the priests of having "set their hearts" on the best places and he described the crowd that was listening resentfully to his parables as "dull of heart". One other memorable saying should be quoted to complete the picture: "Learn of me for I am meek and humble of heart".

Each of these quotations deserves careful attention if ever we are to know ourselves. By the word 'heart' Christ does not mean the brain, the memory, the will, the senses but that personal, conscious, emotional commitment which reveals our inward desires. He did not accuse the crowd of being dull witted but dull of heart. He did not say that those with a clean imagination would see God. Despite all the complexities of the subject, Christ offers to simple people a very simple explanation when he says that it is from the overflow of the heart that the mouth speaks.

Let us, then, enter and examine this inward life of the heart. All that we do in our rooms, on the public stage, in our personal relations; our attitude to sex, to business, politics, art, work, recreation and religion is governed from this central control room, aptly called the heart. Endless attempts have been made to describe this mysterious place. Some, like St Teresa, must fall back on parables, her *Interior Castle* the most elaborate and the most successful, to reveal this inner life. Others, like St Francis de Sales, prefer theological precision, dividing the heart into two main compartments, with two sub-sections in the higher part. Huxley splits the Ego in two, distinguishing in it a creditable and discreditable side. For myself, I am best helped by two concise paragraphs of Dr Sherwood Taylor which I would like to quote in part. Naturally so profound a subject does not lend itself to easy reading but you will find that both passages, taken slowly, will afford us considerable light.

This inner life is lived in a strange enough world; for in truth each man and woman dwells in a different environment—so different that I believe that not two people have so much as half in common. Men know each other's inner world so slightly that they neglect this difference and it is only when two people have a relationship of utter love and trust that their inner lives begin to become perceptible to each other and are revealed as mutually most strange.

What are the constituents of this inner life? First there are memories of men and places and actions, a few pages curiously selected from the countless volumes of experience—curiously selected and strangely distorted, as we find when old memories are confronted with the things remembered. There is a system or, at least, a view of the world constructed from principles whose origin is the thoughts and conclusions of ourselves and others, whether known in the flesh or through their writings; some of these principles being casual and ill-grasped sojourners, others smoothed and hardened by constant use into habits of thought and action. Memories and thoughts may be records of fact or symbols of something within ourselves or both of these; and always in the depths of the mind an unknown agent fashions for us symbols, fantasies, and images which are manifest in dreams but also well up into and tinge the rational thoughts of our waking hours. All these are, as it were, the matter of the mind but there are forces also, loves and hates, the magnetic drawing of the mind to beauty, truth and goodness, of the body to the objects of its desire. Above, within, beyond all these we know the controlling I, who knows that I can decide within ill-defined and uncertain limits what I shall think and what I shall do; Plato's charioteer driving his ill-matched team.

In these fine passages, Sherwood Taylor sketches in outline almost as much as we may ever know by personal effort about ourselves. Rightly he is vague, for a more precise, cut and dried description would not match the confusion which we all know to be there. I like in particular his emphasis on two essential points.

I am glad that he underlines our loneliness. Part of the reason why so many prefer not to think at all, to keep their feet on the ground and both eyes on their bread and butter, is the fear of this loneliness known to be lurking in the centre of the heart. Because each of us is, in a sense, unique, utterly unable to communicate even a fraction of our inner selves to others, we cannot by ourselves, unaided, escape such loneliness. The means of escape will be considered later, it is the fact of loneliness which must now be recognized. We are as isolated as the first, heroic astronauts who set off in sealed capsules to fly alone into outer space. We, too, cut off from the world, sealed inside ourselves, weight-less, full of theories but with no previous practice, must journey on alone. We catch a glimpse of others and they see us through a very small square of glass. Through poetry, art in all its forms, conversations, we may some-times catch a glimpse of another's soul. A sudden flash of insight follows, seconds of sympathy, wonder, ad-miration, shame or horror accompany these fleeting revelations of another's inner life.

Secondly, Dr Sherwood Taylor stresses both the order and confusion of our inner life. Over the years we have acquired a mass of memories, experiences, principles. Of a few we are directly conscious, the bulk lie half-forgotten or forgotten for good. Each of these played its part and vanished after adding its contribu-tion to our mental state. Some of our ideas lie on the periphery of consciousness to be called up if we so wish. "All we know," writes William James, "is that there are dead feelings, dead ideas and cold beliefs and there are hot and live ones and when one grows hot and alive within us, everything has to re-crystallize about it." Thoughts, emotions, experiences are, in one sense, never lost. They go to the building up of that mental background on which the light of consciousness will play. Just as the index of a book or the catalogue of a library records the topics and titles and supplies refer-ence numbers so in our mental background past experiences have been grouped under different heads. If for some reason I say or think the word 'Love' or

'Security', the Capital I may draw from the unconscious background is my accumulated experience on
the required point.

I am mixing metaphors as boldly as St Teresa—perhaps this is the only way to approach such subtle truths.
All our lives have gone to the filing and cataloguing of
experience. Adolescent friendships, lessons from books,
emotional reactions to joy and sorrow, happy memories
of a safe home with devoted parents, all these create
the mental background by which the conscious Ego is
sustained. Sadly enough, less worthy memories are also
there and the loneliness, insecurity, sin, neglect and
cruelty of childhood also leave their deposits in the
unconscious mind. The words 'Our Father' may not
prove so appealing if under the reference in our mental
index is only harshness and cruelty. This unconscious-
ness is truly part of us, bubbling up in dreams, over-
flowing in times of sickness and delirium, providing the
background of experience on which the spotlight of
consciousness may shine.

Consciousness is always in the present moment and
it varies in strength from day to day. In sickness and
fatigue its light is feeble and unsteady while the area
of experience that it plays upon is small. At other times
its beam extends firmly and far further, providing a
wider picture, associating facts long since forgotten,
offering us a more purposeful sweep of life. Consciousness like a spotlight is for ever moving about, searching
for something, and it pauses only when it is satisfied.
Sometimes it hesitates, sometimes it seems uncertain,
lighting up in our mental background two or three
conflicting groups of ideas. Then, of a sudden, it will
hold itself steady, picking out one dominating constel-

lation, presenting these before us for the rest of a lifetime, or, at least, for many years. Psychologists follow
many theories, use many examples, build many hypo-
theses to explain our motives and activities. One may
choose between them or ignore them all. One central
observable fact cannot be ignored.

The Capital I, moving restlessly over the experiences
of a lifetime, seems to be searching for some particular
good. For what is it looking so patiently? Once again it
is Christ who answers the question in simple language
which disguises his astonishing profundity. He says,
"Where thy treasure is, there is thy heart also". Months
of meditation will not exhaust the wisdom of this one
line. Behind and above and beyond the Capital I itself
lies a further reality in which it somehow knows that it
will be satisfied. However incomprehensible the in-
tricacies of our make-up, there is not one of us who
cannot check our inner life on this concrete fact. We
are all the time seeking for our treasure and when we
think that we have found it we will cling to it with
our whole heart. We may recognize this yearning in
ourselves and on every level, this longing for self-
fulfilment and the happiness which will come with it.
Somehow we know ourselves to be incomplete, to be
insecure and changing, moving forward, day by day,
like donkeys, enticed by the carrot dangling before our
nose.

As children we woke up excited every morning,
wondering what each new day would bring. TV com-
mercials play on this fact, picturing the litle ones
clustering round the breakfast table panting for the
new and fullest satisfaction of malt-flavoured, honey-
centred cereals. Next, there was Christmas ahead—or

was it a birthday?—with the thought of presents which we wanted and about which we had dropped innumerable hints. The presents came and went with no more lasting satisfaction than the popcorn to be replaced by sport, pocket money, scholarships, teen-age friends. Next we wanted maturity and awaited so eagerly and with much expectant gossip for the all-satisfying experience of sex. As each goal was reached, its share of experience passed from consciousness to the unconscious to reappear, maybe, in our last delirium, if not before that in our dreams. Each of us has known partial satisfaction, partial self-fulfilment, a treasure which held our hearts for a few weeks, or months or years. The Capital I is still searching, still restless and unsatisfied.

The yearning for self-fulfilment is still with us, showing itself in our inner conversations as we pace the bedroom or examine our faces in the glass. In adolescence there were grounds for hope that something sensational would turn up later, in middle age we begin to fear, deep in our hearts, that it never will. Some turn sour at this basic disappointment and stay disgruntled all their lives. Others accept a purposeless existence, making do with partial satisfaction through study, business and their social life. Some refuse to think at all, surrendering to trivial occupations as a way of 'killing time'. A frightening expression this, aptly describing the melancholy end of so many lives. There are, however, those who remain spiritually young, still aware of their own potential, still sure that this fundamental yearning will be met and satisfied. These, young of heart even in middle age, keep searching for the treasure, knowing from the experience of a lifetime that there is a treasure which the human heart was designed to achieve.

"Where thy treasure is, there is thy heart also." We have Christ's authority to support our treasure hunt. Unlike so many other religious leaders, Christ never missed an occasion to stress the rightness of self-interest on this vital point. Far from condemning it, he went out of his way to praise it, not once but many times: in the parable of the pearl of great price, in the reward of those stewards who traded with their talents and in the repayment of all those who give so much as a cup of cold water in his name. The famous eight Beatitudes are a promise of eight rewards. Is there a single instance in the Gospel story where Christ asked for effort without promising reparation or frowned on those who had followed him for gain? He certainly pointed out the error of those who looked for the false, ephemeral, unsatisfying quick result. The long-term reward which would fully satisfy he stressed time without number, an encouragement to those in middle age who are searching still.

To complete our search for self-knowledge and self-fulfilment we may edge just one step further into the centre of our inner world. Deep in the centre of our heart, in a silent world beyond the reach of the senses and the imagination, the Capital I keeps probing, seeking for self-fulfilment and security. It is alone and working in the dark. For in the centre of our being is a cloud of unknowing, in which even thought itself seems to fade. Dr Sherwood Taylor puts it to us in this way: "Perhaps deeper and less clearly apprehended are certain knowings which are not facts or desires, the knowing and turning to something changeless that is not seen or heard by sense or imagination; something that remains when the tumult of the mind is hushed, when even the I is still and waiting. In this region there are no words, no images but there is that to which every thought and fantasy and imagining and desire are subject."

Can this darkness be God? How many close their eyes in prayer and find this darkness but cannot recognize the God whom they expected there?

taken in his heart. Christ expressed this complex operation in those two sentences, already quoted: "It is from the heart's overflow that the mouth speaks", and "Where thy treasure is, there is thy heart also".

An awareness of these three levels will prove of increasing value as we seek to develop our capacity for life. So many problems come into focus and may be tackled correctly when once we know the level of their attack. Take, for example, prayer. We may reach out to God on all three levels and, hence, there will be three different kinds of prayer. Much more of this in Chapter 7. A knowledge of the same three levels will help us to deal with the perennial worry of distractions in prayer. They also help very much in the task of examining our conscience, about which more in Chapter 6. These same three levels assist us in assessing the cause and nature of lustful desires. Scruples, worries, fears follow a standard pattern, much more easily met and mastered when we know about our own machinery. Nor will we speak so glibly about loss of faith when doubts crop up on the second level of our life. The use of drink and drugs, so hard to restrict when we are working blindly, seems so very much easier to balance as soon as we appreciate their exact effect. Indeed, subjects as far apart as sport, the liturgy, sleep, work and television may all be dealt with in our plan. Most important of all, tension is at once removed when we grasp that a full life turns on a perfect blending, that we must balance our activities on these three planes. Too much emphasis on our life in public will make us trivial and superficial, too much effort at introspection and they will be calling for us with a padded van.

THE TRIALS OF THE DIVIDED SELF

Our own personal experience teaches us that we are liable to conflict at one time or another during the process of balancing our lives. Our activities on all three levels may not synchronize. When we were young and life was lived chiefly on the surface, such conflict was not so easily perceived. As we grow older and the differences between public and private life become apparent, we experience a dislocation between what we do and what we think. Later still, we are more aware of the deeper world within us which, again, seems to contradict the aspirations which we cherish as we pace our rooms. This friction of the divided self may be very painful but far less worrying if we are expecting it. William James helped me very much with this telling sentence: "The normal evolution of character chiefly consists in straightening out and unifying the inner self".

It is encouraging to note that many of the most balanced and helpful of spiritual writers, William James among them, suffered just such a period of acute distress. Indeed James himself was trained as a doctor and turned to psychology after a nervous breakdown had upset his career. Many of the spiritual disturbances which he describes so gently were first experienced in himself. St Francis de Sales, surely one of the most benign of all spiritual directors, suffered a collapse as an undergraduate at Padua. His studies brought him to the subject of predestination, always, for sensitive souls, a source of distress. Without falling into the error of attributing nervous breakdowns to all those who show spiritual leanings, I think that we may fairly recognize the same pattern of unbalance in the spiritual progress of many saints. So St Teresa at the start of her life in the Convent of the Incarnation endured a prolonged and agonizing illness which, from our present knowledge, seems to have been nervous in origin. Ignatius of Loyola passed through a time of considerable tension during his year in the cave of Manresa, much of his suffering based on scruples and caused by enthusiasm. He himself records that he was once tempted to suicide. We have only to read the *Confessions* to appreciate the struggle which Augustine fought inside himself. The effort to straighten out and to unify the inner self may take many years. It is a task which is worth attempting for the sake of interior and everlasting peace. So many of the great saints—I have mentioned only four out of many hundreds—lived at a time when there was less precise knowledge and fought their lonely battle by themselves. We are more fortunate for we may easily profit by their experience. Nothing would be more stupid than to imagine and so induce such spiritual symptoms; each of us is different and I am sure that there must be many saints who escaped such conflict and agony. I cannot think of many such examples for a period of struggle seems to be the lot of most spiritual men.[1]

Whether we endure a great conflict or not, we discover early in our search for self-knowledge the harm which a faulty use of the imagination may cause. Imagination badly controlled may cause endless mischief, making it well nigh impossible to know ourselves or to find God. If we have a wrong impression on these two subjects, the whole balance of our lives will be upset.

Do you recall the simile which I used in the previous

chapter to describe that mental background over which the light of consciousness plays? I there suggested that our previous emotions, thoughts, experiences were filed away in this unconscious background while a reference was entered as in the appendix of a book. If the Capital I for one reason or another requires to draw from memory the summary of past experience on a definite topic, one word is enough to produce the reference to all that has been filed. Say the word 'dentist' and all the memorable, normally painful, details of past visits to various practitioners come to mind. Blood, mouthwash, drill are very pictorially and sensibly represented; I recall the very magazines which I read in the different waiting-rooms and see the outsides of the various houses in which these patient and skilful men practised their nefarious art. Perhaps I am allowing my imagination to run away with me in claiming to recall so many details, but this is done merely to heighten the point.

Now supposing, in just the same manner, we were to say the word 'God'. We each would vary very much as to the impressions of God that we had collected, some of us might have many memories, others few. A great many of our entries might be wrong.

Purely as an imaginative exercise and solely as an example of the impressions collected in a lifetime, let me compile a sample reference card in a mental catalogue. Though largely fanciful, this card was based on the recollections of a living man, henceforward Archie, who called one evening recently to talk about God. I told him about this chapter and he, kindly, agreed to attempt his impressions about God. For the first time in many years, God was evoked from Archie's subconscious world. Archie said the word 'God'. His impressions of God after fifty-four years on earth were summarized thus. He agreed that they came as impressions, much muddled; part word, part sound, part association with other memories. Indeed, the first impression that Archie had was of the archaic language of the Bible and the Parson's voice. Next, Archie thought of 'do-gooders' to the accompaniment of the Royal Choral Society singing the one word 'Counsellor'. Archie's card was not, then, accurate; he had not thought about God for many years. Yet certain facts about God were associated with definite places and could be given approximate dates. We checked it together and it came out in this rough shape:

God. Male. Living in heaven. Tall, bearded. With Abraham, Noah, Moses. Much interested in Noah's ark.
Made Sunday for himself (1914).
Likes night prayers; is looking after Daddy (1916).
Forbids adultery and swearing.
Pleased with David's psalms.
Wicked Communists reject God (1918).
Prayers to him with mother, in school chapel. Prayers answered twice.
O God our help in ages past.
What God hath joined together (1933).
Why I believe or do not believe in God. Four articles in Sunday paper (1936).
Days of National Prayer (1940-45).
God mainly interested in His Holy Will and punishing the transgressor.
Forgive us our trespasses. Amen.

Archie's impressions of God may sound artificial and static for he was racking his brain for my sake who, in

long hand, was trying to write them down. Nevertheless they have an interest and value as a demonstration
of the problems which all must face in the spiritual
life. A great many other people, were they equally
honest, would not want to laugh at Archie or to claim
that their mental impressions were richer than his.
Some, like myself, might possess more information, but
information by itself is of small avail. Information,
further, is often wrong.

In studying Archie's impressions, we see at once why
his Ego, ceaselessly searching for self-fulfilment, cannot
recognize its treasure in God. At best Archie has at the
centre of his heart a bearded image of a superman. His
image of God is unattractive, for who would find peace
with one whose hobbies are limited to punishing the
transgressor and insisting on his own will? Archie's
imagination, fed, alas, by silly people, is playing havoc
with his inner life. Yet Archie has an inner life. He, too,
talks to himself in the bedroom and the bathroom, fears
loneliness, is beginning to experience the frustrations of
a seemingly pointless life. It was, in fact, a feeling of
emptiness which led him to search for self-knowledge
and which brought him to drop in one evening for a
chat. Archie now knows how feeble and false are his
fifty years of impressions about God. It is not too
late for Archie or for any of us who are willing to make
the effort, provided that we are prepared to keep our
imagination under strict control.

THE WRONG USE OF IMAGINATION

One of the greatest obstacles to self-unification is the
wrong use of the imagination than which, to quote the

E

words of Fénelon, "nothing is more opposed not only to the life of faith but also to true wisdom". Yet imagination is a brilliant gift of inestimable value without which the memory would be hobbled and our social life destroyed. The ability to form and to retain images in the brain, to associate ideas, to ordinate the data provided by the senses is the foundation of all conversation and of art in all its forms. Reviewers would certainly be at a loss for words for how often do they describe a novel, a speech, a play, a painting or a piece of music as imaginative. Life would be weary without this warm and endearing talent; an unimaginative man is normally a bore. Actors, especially, must rely on this quality if they are to put themselves into so many different parts. We are all actors on our public level and the more successful we want to be in winning and leading others, the more will our imaginative powers be taxed.

While the merits of imagination may be easily listed, its weaknesses are not so clearly observed. The first of these, so admirably described by Frank Sheed in his *Theology and Sanity*, is found in the substitution of imagination for true, objective thought. How many children have experienced this at school in mathematics classes for the exact sciences require exact thinking and are rarely mastered by the imaginative.

Let me quote Sheed's words.

The first difficulty in the way of the intellect's functioning well is that it hates to function at all, at any rate beyond the point where functioning begins to require effort. The result is that when a matter arises which is properly the job of the intellect, then either nothing gets done at all, or else the imagination leaps in and does it instead. There is nothing to be done with the intellect until the imagination has been put firmly in its place. And this is extraordinarily difficult. One of the results of the fall of man is that imagination has got completely out of hand; and even those who do not believe in that 'considerable catastrophe', as Hilaire Belloc calls it, must at least admit that imagination plays a part in the mind's affairs totally out of proportion to its merits, so much out of proportion indeed as to suggest some longstanding derangement in man's nature.[2]

It will not be out of place at this juncture to recall the warning given in the foreword of this book. The problems connected with the use of the imagination are highly complex and cannot adequately be treated in so short a space. Simple words are so scarce that the very word 'imagination' must be used to cover a wide variety of meanings, to stand service for that association of ideas on which so much artistic genius is founded and also for those subjective fantasies which lead to mental distress. Frank Sheed is discussing imagination in its relationship to thought. One might write whole chapters on the connection between imagination and memory or on the value of imagination in creative art. Only by introducing a great many technical words would it be possible to distinguish one form of imagination from another, condemning what is bad and praising what is good. This is a simple book for simple people and to preserve its nature no such distinctions have been introduced. A great number of very distinguished writers in the past have been satisfied with condemning the wrong use of imagination and the ordinary person almost certainly knows what this implies. Imagination is wrongly used when it departs from objective reality to build up false impressions of an unreal and subjective sort.[3]

Sadly enough, this misuse of the imagination is not always of the patient's doing but may have been taught to him at school. How many children were told then, kindly or less kindly, that they were not intelligent. As a result of such advice, many, from false humility, abandoned all effort to think. They even derided egg-heads and thanked God that they themselves were simple, stupid but honest men. Armed with so good an excuse for not thinking, they next saved themselves all effort by the use of the cliché, "it is a bit above me", and unconsciously accepted imagination as "very much more in my line". They should have been told that there is a great difference between being intelligent and being thoughtful, that a great many intelligent people misuse their imagination while an equal number of not very intelligent human beings are profoundly thought-ful, as all who look may see. Men who give themselves time to think become thoughtful whether they are in-telligent or not. Not all farmers, sailors, night watch-men, invalids are highly intelligent but many are thoughtful because their very profession affords them time to think. On the other hand, a great many seem-ingly brilliant children by the wrong use of imagination allow their intellects to atrophy. Where imagination is substituted for thinking, life ends at the public and private levels and the inner world is deprived of nourishment. Many saints were stupid, any number of them failed or would have failed in the simplest exam-ination, and yet I cannot think of one example of an unthoughtful saint.

Forgive a digression which may prove boring but

which is of lasting importance in the spiritual life. In the case of Archie we see the consequences where a man is not prepared to think. Imagination is curbed only by intellectual effort, a tedious fact which all must face. I cannot grow in appreciation of Shakespeare if I never see his plays or read his scripts. The exquisite joy of great music will never reach me if I am not prepared to listen to it. To take the line that everything is 'above our heads' may mean no more than that we hold our heads too low. We are copying the behaviour of little children who refuse to learn the alphabet because it is so much more easy to scribble with coloured pencils on a pad.

The second threat from the imagination is expressed in the oft used admonition, "Darling, you are just imagining it". Our imagination, if not controlled and constantly checked against the objective facts outside us, will create an unreal world inside our heads. For imagination not only forms mental pictures based on direct, sensible experience but it is further able to sit back and edit a film. A similar operation is seen in a TV studio when a programme is edited. On the central table are jumbled strips of film, a pile of 'stills', charts covered with statistics, pages of suggested dialogue. Technicians fiddle with bulbs and switches to make sure that the programme is presented in what we aptly term 'the right line'. A musical director is lifting snatches of melody from this or that composer that the background music may enhance the scene. From all this available material, the programme producer selects his line. He uses every possible device and gimmick and gadget to 'put this line across'. If a camera cannot lie, the man behind it can. He may flatter or degrade. He makes the selection, cuts, edits and presents his version of the facts. During the war the German and British information services, using the same facts and, often enough, the same photographs, produced contradictory accounts of the identical scene. We, too, are programme editors, but with this subtle difference, for, in our imaginative exercises, we are also the audience. We give ourselves the type of programme that we wish to see. This point was mentioned in a previous chapter where we were compared to author-actors who could write for themselves the leading, romantic parts.

Self-idealization is among the more nefarious of imagination's felonies. This distortion starts in early childhood when the desire for achievement, success, attention is thwarted in any way. Children soon acquire the trick of retiring to view a film of their successes inside their head. Aggressive types see themselves sweeping all before them, the timid imagine themselves as hopeless failures, fit only to be swept away. No true humility causes such self-derision from which a perverted satisfaction is derived.

Next comes the stage of judging others purely on the way that they react to us. "I like him; I do not like her; he is understanding; she narrow-minded" are judgments too often based on prejudice. This very word, so full of pain for ourselves and other people, implies an advance judgment long before the facts are known. There are few more painful or more profitable exercises than the making of a personal list of prejudices. Our standard of values in literature, sport, history, politics and, alas, much of our day-to-day behaviour have been constructed out of the false impressions of an imaginary world.

Many people imagine themselves free of such errors of imagination because they have no conscious pictures in their mind. They know that they are using their imagination when they sit back and re-live the pleasures of their last vacation but the judging of others seems to them a very different exercise. They form no picture of Mrs. Teaspoon when they describe her as a cat. Nor do they carry any fantasies in their mind when they idealize themselves. Imaginative fantasies do their damage quickly and then disappear. All that remains after they have gone is a false impression which, all too often, passes itself off as thought. Thus I may have the impression that the manager is against me but I never trouble to consider how such an impression was first formed. If I was already prejudiced against him, it is very likely that my imagination deliberately misconstrued a trivial act. The phrase "I could read between the lines" conveys exactly the formula to which a false imagination works.

Once we have idealized ourselves, that is, formed an impression of our strength and weakness, imagination forces us to the next disastrous step. Instead of allowing us to devote our effort to our true fulfilment, it encourages us to actualize this false impression of ourselves. The sheer waste of energy is sad enough but the unhappiness which this process may cause to ourselves and others will fall not far short of calamity. To make the situation clear we need only turn to an extreme case.

Probably we have all known girls of no more than average appearance who have romanticized themselves. Secretly they cherish the impression that they are both beautiful and appealing and that every boy

North of the Thames is after them. Their dress, their walk, their conversation, habits and behaviour are all distorted to fit an impression utterly at variance with the facts. They are compelled to lie, to boast, to feign intimate friendships, to consort with people whom they secretly hold in contempt. All the energy of their lives, their capacity for happiness is being wasted on a goal which they lack the means to reach. The bitterness of their private lives increases daily until the strain on their nerves will prove too great. How many a nervous breakdown is a parody of the Gospel precept: "It is from the overflow of the imagination that the mouth speaks". The case of these girls is obvious but, in a more subtle way, the same false impression may be ours. Once, years ago, when I was a schoolmaster, a timid little boy made, inadvertently, a most amusing remark. The class cheered, with disastrous results. The timid little boy formed the impression that he was a humorist. From that day onwards, he could not resist cracking his witty asides. Heaven knows what he is doing now but it would not surprise me if I heard that his life had been ruined by the false impression that he was one of nature's funny men.

Extreme cases are easily seen and great novelists seize them, for they provide a 'real life' plot. So Wilde told the story of Dorian Gray, Locke the tragedy of Jaffery, Cronin, in *Hatter's Castle*, the grim account of a cruel father who drove his little girl to overwork from a wrong impression of his own intelligence. It is, however, not so easy to recognize the symptoms of this self-idealization in the day-to-day decisions of a humdrum life. As easy a way as any is to compose a list of our own imaginary pains, imaginary grievances, imaginary rights, imaginary privileges, imaginary friends and enemies, imaginary fears.

If we collect such a short list of imaginary irritations and frustrations, we may notice how easily they turn —to use Karen Horney's neat expression—into "the Tyranny of the Should". "I should be able to achieve this—I should be treated better—people should make allowances for my headache—they should consult me sometimes—I should have won that scholarship. Why shouldn't I keep them waiting?—I shouldn't have to ask twice—why shouldn't I park my car there if I want?" These and other examples may be summed up in the general expression, "I should be able to achieve in public the image of myself which I have created in my room". The desperate effort to do just this leads to disaster when pushed too far. Come overwork, a sense of failure, the feeling that others are against me, an endless, nagging grievance against life itself.

More will be said about the cure for all this in the following chapters; sufficient here to recognize the dangers and the harm which imagination may cause in our understanding of ourselves. Worse even than this is the damage done in the spiritual order when we discover, horror of horrors, that we have made for ourselves an imaginary God!

The most pernicious of the by-products of an uncontrolled imagination is the false impression of spiritual reality. Spiritual beings, because abstract, cannot be imagined; the senses do not reach them and they must always be unimaginable. With one obvious exception to be mentioned later, no accurate spiritual pictures may be formed. By no effort of imagination are we able to picture a human soul. The same is true of virtues and vices, of sin, devils and angels and, most of all, of God. Where we try to picture the supernatural, we produce little beyond a fairy story and, such is our folly, we come little by little to believe in it. The supernatural world which is hard enough to grasp by unaided reason becomes pure fantasy when imagination takes a hand.

Little children have not yet come to the use of reason when first they are told about God. They picture him as best they may in their imagination, using the bits and pieces which their five senses bring along. They build up an Identikit picture of God as they also build up the likeness of Jack the Giant Killer, and in their simple way grow equally devoted to each. This harmless exercise may one day prove of value when the unconscious theology of the nursery deepens into the conscious convictions of adult life. This presumes that reason will later correct the childish image and that, in adolescence, the child will learn how to use and how to control the imagination which is itself unsuited to spiritual maturity.

You and I were, no doubt, duly warned of the obvious dangers and we nodded our heads to show that the lesson had gone home. But had it? The habit of forming imaginary pictures will never be cured by nodding the head. Even those of us who began to use our reason and to build up a new approach to God based on thinking, probably retained our imaginative impressions as well. We had two views, one imaginative, one thoughtful, running parallel. The thoughtful view is far more difficult to hold where the imaginative one is easy; the thoughtful view proves tedious at times, even boring, where the other entertains. It is colourful, painless, attractive but inaccurate. Those with intellectual courage chose the harder way and by now have progressed much farther, the majority, while abandoning a childish image of Jack the Giant Killer, have retained their childish impression of a fairy-tale God.

We must step lightly with the angels over so delicate a subject which has the capacity to generate considerable heat. Religious imagination is a complicated business which touches on many private preserves. Teachers with their visual aids, publishers brandishing their illustrated Bibles, Italian artists holding aloft their brushes will fall on anyone who disputes their sincerity or their skill. Before we know where we are, we may find ourselves criticizing Fra Angelico or Botticelli whose genius has enriched the world with so many lovely pictures, ravishing but often spiritually absurd. The fault lies not in the masters themselves but in our own untrained imaginations which have usurped the place of thought. Fra Angelico offers us through his skill an interpretation of reverence, sanctity, divinity in three dimensions and in flesh and blood. The effect is uplifting and leads to a fuller realization unless we spoil it by taking it all too literally. Lesser artists than Fra Angelico are less effective, producing a debased image which, in certain ages, matched a debased faith.

In our search for God, we must recognize the fact that imaginative pictures and impressions are not a harmless hobby but a serious impediment. Frank Sheed, as always, states the problem well.

There is no better illustration of a way in which a mental image can still affect thinking even after it has been formally expelled from the mind than the picture of God as a venerable man with a beard rather like the poet Tennyson or perhaps Karl Marx. Nobody who can think at all any longer believes that this is what God is like. But even those who laugh most scornfully at its naïvety, find that they are still dangerously affected by it. It is rather like what happens when we read a novel with illustrations. Without in the least realizing it, we absorb a certain impression of the characters from the way that the artist has drawn them and this impression affects our whole reading of the book. As I have said, the thing is below the level of consciousness. We take it for granted that we have formed our ideas of the characters from what the author has written. We may very well have forgotten even that the book had any illustrations. But their influence abides to colour every judgment. I believe that a sufficiently penetrating analyst could discover some influence of the venerable man with a beard in all that is written about God—even by the most profound and profoundly orthodox of theologians but most notably by the most unorthodox modern thinkers in theology. Among these, for instance, there is a dead set against the idea of a personal God, an idea which their intellects find quite revolting. My own conviction is that they are not revolting against the philosophic concept of personality as applied to God; they are revolting against the venerable old man with a beard. The influence of that long-established image is so great that the moment they begin to think of God as a person, they begin to think of him as that person, so curiously like Lord Tennyson. Naturally they stop at once.

Professor Macmurray is even more blunt than Sheed. He writes: "When therefore a society has crystallized a conception of God which is false, the professed atheist may be more religious than the theist". Nor does this imaginative approach begin and end with God himself. Innumerable spiritual realities have become comic, even ridiculous. The devil is no more real than Father Christmas while angels, for all the skill of Botticelli, seem like Bunthorn's love-sick maidens with wings.

Not only does this faulty use of imagination starve our inner lives by keeping religion on the surface, not only does it prevent the Capital I from seeing God as the only source of true fulfilment, but it may also, by the very stupidity of its phantasms, raise serious doubts against the faith. When people say that they have doubts about the faith, as often as not, like the woman mentioned in the first chapter, they mean that they have doubts about the imaginary pictures of the supernatural life. Some try to brush away such doubts but they hardly escape the problem, for a religion based on imagination breeds imaginary hopes and imaginary fears.

Take a few examples which, I hope, show clearly what I mean. How many I have met whose dread of the Last Judgment is based on the strange impression that they will be tried in a celestial Bow Street with all the free seats in the public gallery occupied by their friends. They are, in fact, far less afraid of God than they are of their neighbours when these hear of their hypocrisy. Again, how many intelligent people are revolted at the thought of bodily resurrection because they have tried to picture it. They have seen paintings of skeletons creeping out of coffins, rubbing their eye-sockets in wonder before setting out to search for their proper toes. Who wants to go to a heaven in which we stand in a choir of mitred bishops for eternity? Van Eyck, for all his genius, is as far from the truth as the Negro Spirituals. Our enemies have described all this as "Pie in the Sky" and, perhaps, much of it is.

Imagination proves utterly unreliable on spiritual subjects and one must check every detail of every impression against objective fact. No need to deny the artistry of the great painters or to forbid to Virgil, Dante or Newman in their thoughts on the hereafter, the liberties permitted to Jules Verne. The fault is in ourselves for, as Sheed pointed out, we ought to be warned of the danger of such illustrations and yet, somehow, we still end up with the venerable old man with a beard.

How delicate is the language of the Scriptures when it conveys, not the physical likeness, but the overwhelming personality of God. It is the human artists who have done the harm with their illustrations, squeezing the Bible revelations into their three dimensional plane. The patriarchs of old lived as we do with their lives on three levels and the Scriptures gain in profundity when we read them in this way. I see no advantage in picturing Jacob wrestling with an angel but his experience was a true one shared by some of the saints in more recent days. His famous ladder need not be pictured as though it had been borrowed from the local builders, yet, again, the story of Jacob's ladder has been matched by the mystics of many a later age.

As always, the Gospels teach an important lesson simply and painlessly. No physical details are provided to aid the imagination in its fantasies. No imaginative clues are provided as to the looks of anyone. In the whole Gospel narrative we find only two small physical details, that the sinful woman had long hair and that the publican Zacheus was small. So, too, in the Old Testament, the majesty of God is expressed with the same economy of imaginable detail, with the same consummate skill. So we have Moses before the Burning Bush, the ascent of the great patriarch into the cloud above Sinai and the protection of the Jews in the desert signified by a cloud in the day and a pillar of fire by night.

The Temple of Solomon was made to God's requirements and decorated with many precious stones and woods. Yet the Holy of Holies itself, the central shrine, was left empty at God's express command. "And nothing was in the ark except the two stone tablets Moses laid up there on Mount Horeb when the Lord made a covenant with the sons of Israel after their escape from Egypt." Here was the difference, for, while the pagan temples were filled with statues representing imaginary idols, the Jews were allowed no representations of the true God.

CHRIST'S LESSON IN HIS PARABLES

In an earlier chapter, two simple expressions of Christ's explained the complex problem of our make-up and now again, in four or five short stories, he affords the one, safe, imaginative setting for the spiritual scene. One gazes with awe at the skill of this extraordinary teacher who could, by the use of metaphor and simile, capture and harness the imagination without giving it its head. He can tell a story in eleven short lines which is simple enough to be grasped by the most stupid of his hearers and yet deep enough to absorb the attention of great scholars over many centuries. The parables of the Sower, the Tares, the Leaven, the Mustard Seed have been understood by both young and old, clever and stupid, men and women, divided from one another by many centuries and living whole continents apart. More important still, these parables have their force on each level of our lives, free from absurdities of human imagination, are so designed that they will lead us in the very centre of our being to search for the true and for no imaginary· God.

It would be out of place to examine all these parables here but it is a pleasure to propose them as the only imaginative solution which is safe. Put a bulb in a glass or grow mustard and cress on your face flannel, as we did as children, and you may watch Christ's explanation step by step. Always for him the insignificant beginning but with a great potential neatly packed into so small a space. An examination of a seed should prove a deep, spiritual experience. So often Christ said that the Kingdom of heaven was within us and he took a seed to show us how so great a mystery might safely be explained pictorially.

There is the splitting and death of the pod itself, the down thrust of the roots, the orderly evolution of stem and leaf and flower, the life of the plant culminating in the slow formation of the fruit. This process continues silently and secretly, hardly needing our attention, assisted by the qualities of soil and rain and sun. He assures us that the parallel between natural and supernatural action is exact.

Within the literary laws which govern the use of metaphor and simile, this picture of a seed growing is by far the best that we shall ever find. How tranquil it is and how reassuring after the feverish, weird and childish pictures which we have often formed for ourselves. Christ's explanation, imaginable and reasonable, places no strain on common sense. Yet it demands from us adjustments if we are to base our spiritual development on the natural course of development of a seed.

Following Christ's teaching instead of our own imaginative picture, we see both ourselves and God in a new light. First, we recognize that in middle age we are none of us past our prime. Cattle may reach their prime at a given moment but the farmer judges his crops by the fruit. Again, no part of life need be pointless, no life need be fruitless, we grow and ripen from day to day. While stem and blossom and leaves will wither and perish, their task has not been unimportant, all their virtue will survive in the fruit.

One sees in this picture a hint, a faint but encouraging explanation of the contribution made by past experience to our present mental state. The Kingdom of heaven is within us, growing as from a seed. In the course of our lives we may expect a transformation great enough to be covered by Christ's example of the change from a seed to a tree. Heaven ceases to be static —a club to which one is admitted if the committee judge one suitable. Rather, it seems a capacity increasing in us day by day. The more we grow now, the greater our contentment then. How many great saints, unconsciously, have demonstrated this growth within them and how many of us, looking back over life, might see the same. Study the growth of Augustine in his *Confessions*, of Paul from his first appearance in the Acts to the last of his letters, Ignatius from the cave at Manresa to his death in Rome as General of a great spiritual army, Thomas More from being an angry young man in London to the tranquillity of prison in those last heroic months. A seed develops slowly and you cannot hurry it.

F

If we follow the picture of the Sower, we must presume that all that has happened to us in the past, all that is ours in the present are explainable only in the light of what lies ahead. In the centre of our hearts most of us are aware of this. In that inner, tranquil world, well beyond the reach of the imagination, we become aware that a newer and fuller life is developing. Some may even be aware of interior senses, of an impression, not experienced in their younger years. Here it is that one starts to comprehend, but without thinking, what Christ meant by the oft repeated word, 'harvest' and 'fruit'.

it to obey her will. At the time I thought that she was teaching me an urgent lesson, one which I could not formulate for fifteen years.

In this clinic was a telephone booth of large proportions, especially designed to help the nervous child. After much enticement, the small girl from the doll's house was persuaded to enter this kiosk. Once inside it, she could see, through the glass panes around her, the other children playing in the nursery. Again she was alone as in the doll's house but now her attention was drawn to the objective world. She was Queen no more. With eyes round with wonder, she followed the antics of the bigger children, building castles in the sandpit, riding the rocking horse, pushing each other about. She watched but would not venture out. Only after a long delay did I spy her experimenting slyly with the door. She would push it a little open but she herself remained inside. No one could help her but herself. Sooner or later her curiosity would prove sufficient to force her to take a grip on her little self. Yes, she emerged at last, inch by inch, pushing the door warily before her and looking back anxiously to make sure of her line of escape. Now she was elaborating no fairy story nor was she any longer the mistress of her own little world. The other children were wholly indifferent to her panic; they did not need her and the task was hers to establish a relationship. Again, she seemed to me to be illustrating an important theory which now, so many years later, I am able to explain. That little girl must now be twenty; I wonder if she has mastered the lesson herself?

The struggles of this nervous child, leaving her world of dolls for the objective world outside her, exactly describes a major step in the spiritual life. At some stage

in our spiritual development we find ouselves compelled to turn outwards and to become as little children
again. Here is a major conversion, a new psychological
birth for middle-aged men. If the task sounds unattractive, the alternative is even more repulsive, to continue
playing in our doll's house, devising our own stupid,
subjective little games. Though the Kingdom of God is
within us, we cannot find it by ourselves. We probe
deep into our hearts only to find this deep, insatiable
yearning with which we cannot cope. We find, at the
best, darkness and, too often, loneliness. The best that
we can do with such ingredients is to create a God to
our own image and likeness and to pray to him. He is
no better than a ventriloquist's doll, echoing our sentiments. Small wonder that so much religious practice
proves frustrating since it is manufactured out of self-
centredness. As I see it now, the choice is either to
become again as little children or to grow old and suffer
the fate of all 'shut ins'.

BECOMING AS LITTLE CHILDREN

On more than one occasion, Christ spoke about our
becoming as little children; once to the Pharisee Nicodemus he suggested that we must be born again. His
primary meaning is clear from the precise context for
he was speaking to Nicodemus about baptism. Rebirth
into the supernatural world is an essential and Christ
makes this very plain. Yet, just as Memling, Constable,
Wedgwood and other masters had a favourite device
which they incorporated into so many of their varied
creations, so God seems to repeat a simple and favourite
pattern in all that he has made. This parallel we have

already seen in the story of the Sower where Christ shows both natural and supernatural sharing the same form of development. No revealed doctrine here and each of us is free to accept or reject it, but many writers have spoken of a second birth on the psychological plane. One might call it conversion and so avoid all possible misunderstanding; call it rebirth and it suits Christ's pattern when he told us to become like children again. One point, at least, is certain, that middle-aged folk do not become again as little children without a profound psychological change.

So comprehensive is this middle-aged conversion that we seem, in extreme cases, to slough off a dead skin. St Teresa did not hesitate to use this very comparison when she linked us with the silkworm which builds its cocoon, sheds its tubular body and takes to the air as a butterfly. Christ put the same in a different form, returning as always to the comparison with nature: "Unless the grain of wheat die, itself remaineth alone. But if it die, it bringeth forth much fruit".

We have to die to self and we all know it; preachers and holy writers have been harping on this theme for many years. Yet, too often, they make the operation sound so painful and psychologically unattractive that most of us feel that we would prefer to stay in our spiritual sties. Reform and conversion are made to appear an agonizing process in which all that is sweet and pleasurable in life must be renounced for good. Why do holy and righteous people stress the negative so much? Why do they beg us to turn from sex, drink, gambling, swearing and other enormities, offering us knitting, cocoa and the Bible as substitutes? To use a modern expression which exactly conveys the meaning, such fervent exhortations leave us cold. We are aware, if we think at all, that so much of this frenzy for reform proves as much self-centred as any of the vices which it sets out to cure. Aldous Huxley observes, and rightly, "that the mortified are in some respects often much worse than the unmortified is a commonplace of history, fiction and descriptive psychology" He swiftly rebukes the puritan mentality, "for stoical austerity is merely the exaltation of the creditable side of the Ego at the expense of the less creditable. Holiness on the other hand is the total denial of the separative self."

Should any reader begin to suspect that his author is lax, let him stay his condemnation to the end of the present book. Christ seemed to emphasize that we should become again as little children, a conversion far more exacting and far more joyful than converting ourselves into Pharisees. Violent reforms throughout history have rarely, if ever, produced the required results. Indeed, those who are attempting to actualize their idealized selves often make the most vigorous reformers, imposing on themselves and others a standard of behaviour which cannot and, indeed, should not be observed. 'The Tyranny of the Should' drives many selfish people to impose their views on others, to assign burdens, to judge severely on a false scale of values compiled by their idealized selves. It is vital, here, to note that Christ's enemies, now rightly judged the most contemptible in history, accused Christ himself of being lax. They charged him with breaking the Sunday laws, mixing with the wrong type of people, taking a lower standard than St John the Baptist, and, astonishingly, of drinking too much.

With the example of the small girl in the telephone booth before us, let us consider the process of becoming as little children again. In its opening stages it often affords a radiant experience, filled with relief and satisfaction and, on the side, not a little fun. Nor should we forget that where little children ruin their tender lives by ambition and faulty imitation, we in middle age have learned our lesson, having made this mistake once already. It is very much easier to be a little child at forty than at fourteen. No strain is needed, certainly no violence, and the surrender of self brings with it an indescribable relief.

SENSITIVE AWARENESS

Let us be entirely realistic; a genuine emotional awareness of the world outside us is the first step towards a permanent cure. We must go back to start again with those five senses whose first messages to us in childhood were faultily decoded and thus misunderstood. Then, they were heeded, ignored, edited or discarded to fit our small, subjective games. Now, they must be given their true value, whether or not they suit our plans. These five senses remain our one certain link with the world outside us and though they are now older, less alert, possibly a little disillusioned, yet they still present a true objective picture if only we will use them properly.

As I see it, we must first be prepared to waste our time. Away with the overcrowded schedule, itself a symptom of self-importance, a sign that we see ourselves as supermen. We must sacrifice a little time, surrendering to the senses, not thinking but feeling the world as it really is. The little girl gazing from the telephone booth at the world outside her was not, in fact, wasting her time. She was learning to live. We, at her age, also tried to learn this lesson; if it is now forgotten, we must sit down and start again.

When that legendary oldest inhabitant was asked how he filled his day, he gave the classic answer, so often quoted, so rarely followed today. He said, "Sometimes I sits and thinks and sometimes I just sits". We, too, must just sit. We watch the world, not to collect material, to utilize facts, to evolve theories, to pose and answer questions, but to become one with the world of sense through eye, ear, touch, taste and smell. One has but to undertake this exercise for ten minutes to grasp that the solution of our problems is at hand. The strain of life drains out with our self-importance when we mess in with the Universe and abandon our individual pose.

The point that I am trying to make is of such importance that I would like to put it to you another way. No doubt you have seen tourists or been tourists and will recognize travellers of two contrasting types. A great many tourists are self-important and self-conscious, racing round Europe with a motive and a plan. They want to improve themselves, to educate themselves, to enjoy themselves, to broaden their outlook, to add to the number of topics about which they may assert themselves. It is of vital importance to them to visit more places than any of their neighbours and to return with some new gadget which no one else in Ealing or Streatham has ever seen. For some strange reason they despise all other tourists, especially their fellow countrymen. They even develop a grievance if the said fellow countrymen chance to be staying in the same place as themselves. They say, "Hang it all; we came abroad just to get away from them".

Their subjective urge is so unreasonable that they attempt in twenty-four hours to suck in all the history, culture, social life of a city which has been thriving for a thousand years. So they mug up the guide-book, do the Cathedral in ten minutes, race round the Art Collection—"You do this side, Darling, and I'll do that". They must visualize the plan of the town, eat at the most famous restaurant, visit the shopping centre, photograph each other in front of some historic mass of statuary. Then there are the postcards to be bought and written as proof to their stick-in-the-mud neighbours that they are hardened travellers who love to wander far afield. Car stickers are needed, luggage labels and, of course, souvenirs. All these activities are attempted to a background noise of querulous conversation for they must for ever be reminding each other that their next hotel is four hours' hard driving away. Poor dears, they feel so up-to-date, so well-informed, so travelled; why, they even patronize the natives, joking together at their quaint ways.

There is another type of traveller who, because he knows how much he himself is lacking, sets off on his search for enjoyment with no ambitions and but a rudimentary plan. He wanders about. For hours at a stretch, he strolls the streets or sits at a café table, sipping wine. He loves the wine for its essential excellence. With it he drinks in the history of the city and the noise, the life, the bustle of its streets. He senses reality, feels in his heart the beauty of the buildings, shares the joys and sorrows of every passer-by. He loves the Con-

tinent and appreciates its beauty only because he loves
and appreciates life. Now both these types of traveller
have an interest, the one type in themselves, the other
in objective life. The hectic pair would double their
enjoyment if they could persuade themselves to sit
down, forget themselves and relax.

The theory of life which I am striving to defend, a
theory which leads to true spiritual progress, is most
admirably set out by Professor John Macmurray in a
passage which I would like to quote in full. Macmurray
writes:

But when we use our senses just to become aware of
what is around us for the sake of the awareness itself, we
use them in a different and a fuller way. We can look
at things for the joy of seeing them; we can listen to the
sounds of the world because it is good to hear them,
without any ulterior motive or special purpose. In that
case, we look at things not because we want to use
them but because we want to see them. We touch
things because we want to feel them. Sensitive awareness becomes then a life in itself with an intrinsic
value of its own which we maintain and develop for
its own sake, because it is a way of living, perhaps the
essence of all living. When we use our senses in this
way we come alive in them, as it were, and this opens
up a whole new world of possibility. We see and hear
and feel things that we never noticed before and find
ourselves taking delight in their existence. We find ourselves living in our senses for love's sake for the essence
of love lies in this. When you love anyone you want
above all things to be aware of him more and more completely and delicately. You want to see him and hear him,
not because you want to make use of him but simply
because that is the natural and only way of taking de-

light in his existence for his sake. That is the way of love and it is the only way of being alive. Life, when it is really lived, consists of this glad awareness. Living through the senses is living in love. When you love any thing, you want to fill your consciousness with it. You want to affirm its existence. You feel that it is good that it should be in the world and be what it is. You want other people to look at it and enjoy it too. You want to look at it again and again. You want to know it, to know it better and better, and you want other people to do the same. In fact, you are appreciating and enjoying it for itself and that is all that you want. This kind of knowledge is primarily in the senses. It is not of the intellect. You don't want merely to know about the object; often you don't want to know about it at all. What you want is to know *it*. Intellectual knowledge tells us about the world. It gives us knowledge *about* things, not knowledge *of* them. It does not reveal the world as it is. Only emotional knowledge can do that. The use of the senses as a practical means of getting knowledge is thus not a way of knowing the world at all, but only of knowing about it. The wider use of the senses for the joy of living in them, is knowing the world itself in and through emotion, not only by means of the intellect. This is not to disparage intellectual knowledge but only to insist that it is meaningless and without significance, apart from the direct sensual knowledge which gives it reality. One cannot really know about anything unless one first knows it. Intellectual awareness is egocentric. It uses the senses as an instrument. But direct sensual awareness has its centre in the world outside, in the thing that is sensed and loved for its own sake. There is a drawing of George Morrow's which illustrates the difference humorously. It shows a couple standing on a hilltop watching a sunset. The sky is aglow with bars of bright clouds. "What a lovely sunset," the woman says to her husband. "That reminds me," he answers. "Do remember to tell our landlady that I like my bacon streaky."[1]

This powerful passage, which will release its full meaning only on the third or fourth reading, seems to me to express the facts of life most accurately. Much of its doctrine may already be known to us in theory and some of us, wisely educated, may already have rejoiced in its effects. In rural societies emotional awareness is far more acute than in the large, industrialized states. Commerce and competition tend to turn life into a scramble, forcing us to use our senses purely as a means to an end. Such an end is, often enough, promotion, ambition, self-glorification, not the joy of life in itself. How sad to watch children making, and even being taught to make, the first wrong steps. We in middle age have to re-learn the joy of emotional awareness while the children to whom it is natural learn to twist and distort themselves.

As with the little girl, moved from the doll's house to the telephone kiosk, sensitive awareness must be for us the first step. We must surrender to curiosity about the strange world outside ourselves. All that is needed is a shift of interest. Directly we succeed in forgetting to ask. "How can I use this? Will it be useful to me?" we may easily fit ourselves into the world of sense. Religiously-minded people often prove the more timid, for the very expression 'surrender to the senses' sounds to them very much like sin. By an unhappy accident, sense is now linked with sensual and sensual with sex. A morbid preoccupation with sex, so marked a feature of our present society, makes it well nigh impossible to speak about love or to write about the senses without setting off, for some, a chain of erotic thoughts.

Spiritual writers often warn us to guard our senses and we, if not they themselves, seem to misunderstand the phrase. Biographers also love to relate of a saint as loving as St Bernard, that he walked all day by a beautiful lake without gazing at it once. Their implication in this yarn suggests that St Bernard thought such pleasure sensual. A far more likely solution in the case of so great a mystic is that Bernard was in union with a far more lovely reality. In this question of the senses we should recall Christ's specific teaching that evil does not start outside and work its way inwards, it is manufactured in the heart itself.

First, then, we must cultivate this sensitive awareness as the first step towards a reasonable life. What is a reasonable life? It would be an amusing and profitable exercise to write down in a sentence what we understand by the word 'reasonable'. A great many people shy at the word and avoid it for life. Some identify it with a high I.Q., associate it with the oddities of egg-heads and, with false humility, accept the fact that they themselves are unreasonable. Others take it to mean tolerance and common-sense as in the expression, "Darling, do be reasonable". Consult the logic books and you discover that it is reason that distinguishes man from all other animals. A man, they say, is a rational animal and he shows his reason in his power to think abstractly, to adapt means to an end, to cook his food. We are the only animals who cook. The full meaning of reason goes very much further than the stove. Professor Macmurray defines reason as "the capacity to behave consciously in terms of the nature of things which are not ourselves". Put more briefly, it is our capacity for objectivity. No other animal consciously bases his behaviour on the nature of the world outside himself.

REASONABLE BEHAVIOUR

This definition requires considerable thought. If reason is that quality which marks me off as a man, then I should be proud to use it accurately. And if reason is the capacity to act according to the nature of the things outside me, then emotional awareness will prove essential to provide the salient facts. I must be aware of the objects outside me if I am consciously to adapt myself to them.

Reasonable behaviour must be our second step in our escape from self. A new dignity comes into life when we show a reasonable respect towards even inanimate objects. Though these are not alive and have no rights, they are yet wonderfully endowed. Solomon in all his glory was not clothed more beautifully than the lilies of the field. Sticks and stones gain and lose nothing by our behaviour, we it is who find self-satisfaction and self-fulfilment in our reasonable treatment of inanimate life. Respect for one's material is the mark of the genuine craftsman just as lack of it is the sure sign of the oaf. Can it be that a black-coated civilization saps the reason of its citizens by depriving them of the chance to fashion beautiful things? The unreasonable use of materials is not a sin against these but a sign of weakness in ourselves. On the other hand, behaviour, consciously adapted to the nature of the material, is a sure way of escaping from ourselves.

Many egocentric people find an increasing difficulty in adjusting their behaviour to fit the objective world.

Little by little they grow more and more unreasonable and their lives are set to the melancholy melody of a never-ending grouse. Thus, the motorist nurses a sense of grievance if he is stopped by the traffic lights. Golfers break their clubs in temper, housewives turn nasty when the milk overboils. I have seen a bowler-hatted executive kicking the side of the compartment as the train ran into a London terminus late.

Others ignore the nature of their own bodies, smoking and drinking too much, driving too fast, overworking, staying up too late of an evening, reading in a poor light. Others, again, improvise on the spur of the moment, as when a sluttish housewife wipes the tea-pot on the window curtain because she cannot be bothered to find a more suitable cloth. So much unpunctuality stems from an unreasonable attitude to the nature of the world outside us, we fool ourselves that we are supermen who, when we want, can work with such swiftness that we can accomplish a double stint in half the time. Such styles of behaviour are common but they are also petty, childish and unreasonable. Once I become emotionally aware of the objects with which I am dealing, I will respect the laws by which these are bound. At least I should start by not blaming the world outside me when, through my own unreasonable behaviour, my plans go awry.

Once, on a London bus, my neighbour suddenly decided to refuel his cigarette lighter; he produced a capsule of petrol and bit off the end. He squeezed the tube with so much vigour that two thirds of the spirit missed the hole in the lighter and soaked his fingers and the outer case. Yet he was furious when the flint would not spark on the first occasion and still more angry when the next attempt produced a burst of flame. Puffing and slapping to discourage the flame and to save the entire bus from destruction, he shouted in my direction, "Blast, this is always happening to me!"

If we turn from this foolish man to the more important question of religion, we discover that many of our difficulties spring from an unreasonable approach to life. Take, for example, our attitude to God. Many of us start life with a ready-made hypothesis. Some have already decided that there is a God, others that there is not. Our prejudice came from a book or was taught to us by our parents or was acquired to annoy them or to please a much admired friend. I admire Joe, and as Joe is an atheist I must be an atheist as well. It is natural for us in early life to accept the theories taught by those who love us but there should come a moment when we decide to test and to prove the theory for ourselves.

Armed with our hypothesis, we set out manfully to prove it, partly by subjective observations, partly with the aid of secondhand arguments culled from selected books. If few Christians heed the words of intelligent atheists, how few atheists will consider with attention the brilliant writings of the great Christian apologists. No, we already have our hypothesis and seek confirmation for it, not objective truth. With such a mental attitude, we approach the five celebrated proofs for God's existence and these will prove the fact or fail to prove it according to our point of view. C. S. Lewis describes this operation well, for the argument which proved God's intelligence to him as a Christian proved the opposite when he was an atheist. On so vast a field

G

as this, plenty of secondhand facts may be found to bolster either side.[2]

HOW TO FIND THE WORLD

Many of the massive problems concerning God and his existence come from our own unreasonableness. We start out with a theory and with prejudice. Next, we may have the phantasm of the venerable old man with a beard. We also enjoy a sense of our own inadequacy which tends to force us to accept opinions expressed by far more learned men. We may easily accept such opinions and persuade ourselves that we thought them out for ourselves.

If we are Christians, we then make a bee-line for all that is lovely in nature, daffodils, lady-birds, stars, sunsets, bluebells dancing in the woods. A kind, merciful, intelligent God made all these lovely things. Should we, by chance, be pagans, off we streak to compile a dossier of earthquakes, floods, hurricanes, cruelty and disease. Whichever side we chance to support, we select enough material to serve as a substitute for the whole truth. The penalty for this will be paid in full later in our lives. The faith of the believer, built on rickety foundations, is steadily undermined. He finds it harder and harder to fit his image of a kind God with the very harsh facts of life. The disbelief of the atheist prepares him for a still more melancholy end. Writes William James, "The purely naturalistic look at life, however enthusiastically it may begin, is sure to end in sadness. This sadness lies at the very heart of every merely positivistic, agnostic, or naturalistic scheme of philosophy."

Take the extreme and tragic case of devoted parents when their little son is killed in an accident. How often one has heard words of great bitterness in such a crisis: "No, I believe in nothing; a good God would never have allowed such a thing to happen to us". Obviously, the deep distress of the moment must be allowed for but, nevertheless, such indignation is unreasonable. It is not based on an awareness of the world outside ourselves. It stems from a false picture of God, from a faith based on wishful thinking, from an unwillingness to face objective fact. The whole problem of pain derives from this wrongful attitude. If our only standard of judgment is to be "how does this affect me?", then we are doomed to serve a God made to our own image and likeness or to fall back on an empty, agnostic formula of good and bad luck. Take the first alternative and you are forced into the ridiculous position that all good things come from a loving God while the tragic and the painful are entirely due to man. The other choice leads us to a position still more foolish, that life is an accident.

The escape from this dilemma is a sensitive awareness of the world outside ourselves. Instead of collecting facts to prove a thesis, we must achieve contact with the world of objective reality. I become aware at once that objects are not good or bad because they please or displease me. My likes and dislikes are manufactured by myself. Next, I discover through emotional awareness that I myself and the world outside me are subject to a rigid law. It is an arbitrary law from which nothing material is exempt. Miracles excepted, and these are far more rare than many would imagine, the laws of chemistry and physics have all nature taped.

No matter how far the astronauts may fly, no matter what new planets they find and conquer, physics, chemistry, biology, astronomy and the other sciences will eventually be able to express their nature in a formula.

My awareness also tells me that every creature, even the spiders, flies and mosquitoes, are governed by a network of rules. When Christ remarked that we could not add a hair to our heads or an inch to our stature, he was stating a clear and observable fact which awareness will prove. Silvikrin may give me a miraculous head of hair but there is, in fact, no miracle about it, no lotion will ever upset the laws of nature but merely apply them through a formula. My tissues are wearing out according to another formula, which the bright-eyed boys in the laboratories may check. Every detail of the physical life of all of us is governed by nature's law.

A sense of true subjection to these laws of nature will lead to a genuine act of humility. Marcus Aurelius, the good pagan, expressed just this. Further, the common fate shared by all creatures provides a bond between us, that 'we-are-all-in-this-together' type of spirit which produced so much love and heroism in the London blitz. Such lessons as these cannot be learned from books. It is less a question of acquiring information, more a matter of awareness that we are all bound hand and foot by the natural law. Those who have been gravely ill in hospital and have shared the hopes and sorrows and love of other patients, know a good deal more about life than those who confine themselves to Wordsworth's Daffodils. An awareness of this common suffering prevents them from seeing the world through critical, scheming, self-important eyes.

Some religiously-minded people conduct their lives on the hope of divine intervention to exempt them from physical laws and their consequences. The prayer of these people is an endless litany of material requests. Those who believe in God must accept the fact that God may intervene if he wants at any minute, but the evidence that he often does so is slight. True, Christ said, "Ask and you shall receive", but the accumulated wisdom of his life, his speech, his behaviour gives little support to the belief that God will grant such material requests. In one famous passage, he cited the example of an earthly father who does not give to a favoured son gifts which would be bad for him. An awareness of the life outside ourselves may well persuade us that our self-fulfilment will not be obtained by exemption from the common lot of men. There is gigantic relief to be had by accepting our physical bondage without whimpering. Satan's lie to Adam and Eve in the garden was in the form of just such an escape. "Thou shalt not die," he said to them and they believed him; they were our ancestors! Few, today, would be foolish enough to deny death but many fool themselves that they may escape the more irksome and painful of its consequences. Wisdom is born when we are humble enough to accept and even to welcome the common lot. Then, the pagans will say with Marcus Aurelius, "Everything harmonizes with me which is harmonious to thee, O Universe. . . . O Nature, from thee are all things, in thee are all things, to thee all things return." Christians manage in four words to express the same grand submission more fully and far better. Addressing their Father in heaven they say together, "Thy will be done".

As soon as we turn from theory to this sensitive awareness, we know the objective world as it truly is. Whether there is a God or no God, we may entertain no doubts about nature's laws. Submission to these laws drains all the pride from us, class distinctions, subjective fancies and conceits. We are more ourselves and so very much more grateful and more pleasant when we accept physics and chemistry reasonably.

But the same awareness of the objective world which teaches us submission also presents us with a reality which is not bound by the natural law. We become aware of beauty in its many forms. One striking feature of middle age is a heightened awareness of loveliness. The young also admire beauty and art but their appreciation is haphazard, they are tied by convention, by ambition, by the dictates of the fashionable crowd. They tend to judge a painting or a piece of music entirely by its effect on them. How much prejudice enters into artistic judgments at any age.

As we grow older, we are able to shake ourselves clear of such conventions and to become aware of artistic skill, insight, beauty in a tense, almost agonizing way. Novelty means less and we are happy to return again and again to Florence, Toledo, Bruges or Cambridge; to take up again the favoured novels and poems of a lifetime, to start at the very beginning again. One meets people for whom Georgian domestic architecture has become a dominant satisfaction though they know nothing of its history and have never troubled to learn the scientific rules. One such friend drives in his car each evening after dinner to sit before the Georgian façades in Queen Anne's Gate. Others whom I know come to love a certain town, a particular view, the moods of the sea, the tints of the sunset so that they are almost beside themselves with anguish if they miss it and quite carried out of themselves when the chance occurs. Their very faces grow young, their voices change their note, they become like children, seeing beauty in the form which has come to mean most to them. Professor Macmurray quotes the remark of a woman writer who so loved music that she said that she found herself listening to it with the soles of her feet. Adds the Professor sombrely, "If you have any inkling of what that means, you will understand when I say that we have to learn to live with the whole of our bodies, not only with our heads. If we do this, we shall find ourselves able to act in the world with our whole bodies and our actions will be spontaneous, non-mechanical and free."

His point is valuable on two scores. Such an emotional surrender to art provides one of life's richest and most enduring satisfactions but it also carries us a great deal further towards our goal. For in art we become aware of universal life, not tied by any scientific formula. Human genius alone arises above any formula. Shakespeare's eyes and ears and brain were all subject to the physical laws of nature but his Hamlet is not tied. Hamlet is universal, composed by the genius of the poet out of little bits of you and me.

Awareness of art leads us to an awareness of other human beings, each with a body which is bound by the laws of nature and a spirit which is his own. God or no God, proof or no proof, I am aware of these simple facts.

Now the little girl in the telephone booth in Glasgow changed from the wishful thinking of the doll's house to gaze out on the world of men. She was on the threshold of a great discovery which we have taken so many years to assimilate. God or no God, proof or no proof, our sensitive awareness makes us directly conscious of our fellow men.

5

THE PERSONAL APPROACH

BOTH for the author and for the reader, this must be the most exacting chapter of the book. We have now reached that vital contact between human beings towards which all previous chapters have been leading and from which we make our final ascent to God. To make the going harder, charity has now become an uncongenial word. In the course of the centuries, it has switched its meaning, now offering a very diluted version of the virtue which we all need so much. There is, too, a further problem for the author; true charity may only be described by its practitioners, of whom he is not one.

The duty of charity towards our neighbours, so often extolled by worthy, even wordy preachers, has become for many of us both tedious and banal. The jargon we know by heart. We are all familiar with the clichés which draw the cash from our breast pockets without touching or firing the heart. Our money, we know, is needed for one good cause or another and duty forces us to give. Here is just another Christian duty to be written into our heavenly expense account. It makes the subject no more attractive when each succeeding preacher ends his appeal with the reminder that "God is love".

If our language were richer in philosophic words, we could vary the shades of meaning without harming the true sense of charity. As it is, and Aldous Huxley states it fairly, "the word Charity has come, in modern English, to be synonymous with almsgiving".[1] Huxley would have maintained that such a confusion is not entirely innocent. By thus linking charity with cash, our ancestors were able to dodge its fuller implications, easing their conscience with the bland assurance, "We have done our duty, we have given them £5".

Charity having changed its name to almsgiving, 'love', that ever willing skivvy, has had to add another shade of meaning to its heavy load. Love is the hardest-used word in the English tongue. It must cover the behaviour of boys and girls at the back of the movies, the devotion of Damien to his lepers, Lady Chatterley, the ecstasy of a hermit contemplating God. Comes the final insult when someone says, "Gee, I love blanc-mange!" Small wonder that, when we are asked to love our neighbours, we feel slightly cynical.

The escape from cynicism becomes possible when we leave the words behind us and return to the situation in which we find ourselves. The little girl in the telephone booth shows us the choice before us, either our own private life in a doll's house or a relationship with flesh-and-blood human beings outside ourselves. Either we play our subjective games with our neighbours in the role of puppets or we force ourselves to grasp the importance of human relationships. Many people at varying times make a valiant effort to reach others, but at the first sign of failure, they hastily retreat into themselves. I would not mind betting that that little girl ran back for protection to her doll's house as soon as she discovered that the children in the playroom had minds and ambitions of their own. By such a flight, she may have persuaded herself that she was hurting and punishing the others, later she would have discovered, as we must, that she herself was the loser in the end.

Charity becomes tolerable when we discover that it is not a work of supererogation but a cold necessity. One starts being truly charitable when one finds that it pays. Scrooge had to learn his lesson and so must we. My neighbour may not be particularly lovable but the only alternative is an eternity by myself. Righteous Christians may look down their spiritual noses at so mercenary a motive, but Christ came back to it again and again. At least he made it very clear that we had to lose our life to find it and that we could expect in mercy and forgiveness no more and no less than we are prepared to give. Such smug expressions as "I keep myself to myself", "I am indebted to no one", "My home is my castle" are the first steps towards chronic misery. The only escape from subjective loneliness here on earth and, possibly, hereafter is to love my neighbour as myself. Charity in the first stage turns on no virtue in my neighbour but on a change of attitude in myself. So inherently egoistic are we that we will come to look on charity with favour only when we see that our neighbour gets far less out of it than we do ourselves.

Needless to say, the first step towards charity can never be that futile, imaginative exercise of picturing my neighbour as lovable inside my head. Nor is it very much use to prescind from his unattractiveness by imagining that I can see Christ in his place. There may be a few who can maintain such a pose, and very good luck to them, but how can we establish a true relationship with our neighbour if we are pretending that he is somebody else? We cannot fool him even if we fool ourselves. We may be dripping Christian honey but he will dismiss us as pious hypocrites. How much so-called charity adds up to little more than acting on our public level because we think—and wrongly—that Christ has assigned to us so anaemic and artificial a role. It is from the overflow of the heart that the mouth speaks, so our relationships with our neighbours must be very deeply felt.

SENSITIVE AWARENESS OF MY NEIGHBOUR

No, we must begin the other way round with sensitive awareness of our neighbours, of which, I fear, you must by now be piously sick. I cannot have any sort of relationship with my neighbour until I am aware of him. I must be aware of him in full, not just aware of his mannerisms, his silly smile, his affectations but of his life on all three levels, a life so very much like my own. Here is the true challenge of charity, demanding patience, ingenuity and tact. Just as two dogs, many yards apart, suddenly tense their muscles, prick their ears, sniff and drool and whimper as they become aware of one another, so two human beings will tend to bristle at the start. In trains and buses, on the beaches, even in the sorrow of the dentist's parlour, we glare at each new arrival as though he were an aggressor, leper or impostor, a certain threat to our security. We are sure that his toothache is not as bad as ours, that he has muddled his appointment and is now trying to jump the queue. Dogs take less time to accept each other but, then, they are not rational as we.

Sensitive awareness of other human beings is acquired through all five senses, not merely by judging people on what they say. In sophisticated society, conversation is too often studied and a great many speak for effect. We have to be ready at the start to make certain allowances, based on a working knowledge of ourselves. To judge others on appearances is to invite them to judge us by our face. Besides, our aim in our awareness of others is not to use them, to catalogue them, to decide whether or not we wish to know them, but to discover them as they are in themselves. As human beings they are our equals and because they are a match for us, they are also capable of becoming friends. It is surprising the number of people who dislike their equals for fear of them. They avoid their neighbours and seek consolation with their pets. They say, "My dog is such a wonderful companion," as, indeed, most domesticated animals must be. My dog does not argue with me or contradict me nor will he ever lose his trust and confidence. So long as I feed him and pat him, I may count on his admiration no matter how self-centred I happen to be. My neighbour proves a very different proposition, for he has a mind of his own. Not all who keep pets are egocentric but those who love their pets and do not love their neighbours may have matter on which to meditate.

We start, then, with awareness of our fellow men. The casual handshake is not sufficient, we have to know them and sense them as they are. We are not seeking to use them, to win them, to organize or improve them but to be one with them. From such a genuine awareness, which is always outward-looking, will stem that noble relationship which we call personal. The nature of this bond is woven into the very texture of all language for what is language but an interchange between persons, expressed through the personal pronouns and adjectives. I talk to you about him, her, it or them. We say of a friend that we have much in common and by this we mean that we view reality in the same way. Should we share an appreciation of Shakespeare, the poet acts as a type of telstar, passing messages between my friend and myself. Such a union of two persons is established and maintained by such an interest shared. This is very clearly seen in the home where the love between a man and his wife is made visible in their children, but the same relationship may be seen in those whose love for one another is conveyed through a common cause, a common loyalty, mutual appreciation of art or leisure or work. Without the third person singular or plural, the first and second persons would find it hard to communicate. Language matches reality and the personal pronouns hold an honoured place in the growth of charity.

Go a step further in our awareness of other persons and we see how the word 'personal' is often used carelessly. Along with other similar words—'friendly' and 'unfriendly' are examples—'personal' must connote a relationship. When we speak about our personal notes, a personal opinion, personal laundry, we are using 'personal' in place of 'private' and, in so doing, damaging its sense.

PERSONAL FRIENDSHIP

To understand personal relations, we have to return to the three levels on which we live. Corresponding to these three levels of life will be, in our outward dealings, three relationships.

First, in my public life on the world's stage, I will form social relations with those who meet me in society. If I join a club, a bank, a trade union, a political party, I join with others in sharing a common convenience. We are individuals who come together for a common purpose, be this Golf or Glee-singing or Bridge. We make no personal demands on one another and we are united only in sharing the same advantages by observing the same rules. Each of us voluntarily surrenders certain liberties that life in society may be maintained. This is the world in which birds of a feather normally flock together, a world in which we decide whom to know or not to know socially. In this world, too, we run our 'socials' at which we use our acquaintances for a variety of ends.

When I leave this social world for my bedroom or bathroom, I cut myself off from human relationships. This is my private life. It is not strictly correct to call it my personal life though we often do so, 'personal' here meaning the life proper to me. There may be some justification for this use, for when I am alone and free of social conventions I am, in a sense, more myself and more at home. Yet I am sharing nothing with another person, a relationship on which human happiness must rest. Great sorrow may result from this. There is tragedy too, if, as a result of ignorance, a person deliberately schools himself to such loneliness. How often one meets a person whose pride it is never to show any feelings in case he or she should give himself or herself away. The fear of giving ourselves away, of betraying ourselves, of letting the cat out of the bag or the skeleton out of the cupboard forces us to share the fate of the Lady of Shalott. It comes as a shock when we discover, too late, that we have made ourselves 'shut in' and lonely, that true charity consists not in helping other people but in giving ourselves away. The Pharisees ended as humbugs but, perhaps, they did not start there; the word Pharisee means Separate.

I have, then, social relations in my public life, solitude in my private life and personal relations in the centre of my heart. These personal relationships spring from that central point of personal energy already described. Perhaps you can recall from a previous chapter that deep, personal, inner craving lying beyond the Ego which not even an imaginary picture of God will ever satisfy. This yearning receives the first, faint promise of fulfilment in true personal relationships. If we are utterly honest with ourselves, we are forced to admit in deadly secret that we all yearn to love and all yearn to be loved. We want to be appreciated and to appreciate. Not any form of appreciation will satisfy our basic need. I may appreciate Georgian architecture but bricks and banisters cannot respond. I appreciate my dog and he appreciates me but for insufficient motives, he licks my hand but with no knowledge of my inner life. The lick of a dog is poor compensation when placed beside the love of my fellow men. In the relationship with other human beings, I experience a satisfaction which no other earthly substitute may ever replace. The love of the lowest human being exceeds that of the gentlest retriever with tears of emotion in its soft, sub-human eyes.

In true personal relationships, you give yourself away. You are not seeking to extend your influence, to enforce your will, to satisfy a social instinct but to share all that you have with your equals because this is the only way to happiness. Small wonder that, in every attempt to describe such a personal relationship, the human mind tends always to use the language and imagery of courtship or of married love. Who would doubt that in a truly happy marriage one finds the perfect example of human relationship. Yet imagination hurts us here as in so many other subjects; the union between persons may soar very much higher than the intimacy of sex.

Personal relations start with a sensitive awareness of and an interest in others for their own sakes. Next, men being reasonable creatures, we begin to adjust our behaviour to the nature of other persons outside ourselves. We know less of the nature of stones or flowers than of our fellow human beings for the last named share a common nature with ourselves. We find ourselves forced to admit that other human beings are our equals, not necessarily in learning, wealth or social graces, but in the human nature which we share. Fellow human beings enjoy the same rights, duties, aspirations as we have ourselves. To make contact with them, I must adjust my behaviour to provide them with sufficient personal scope. Every human being needs personal breathing space. Learned men have set out the reasonable conditions for all such personal relationships. Pope John XXIII, one of the most lovable of men, writing about the dangers of State interference, insists that a human being should be able to think for himself, free of undue pressure, to initiate action, to assume responsibility and so to fulfil himself.

There cannot be a personal relationship without

H

some recognition of rights and duties similar to these. There will be no personal relationship based on patronage. No common bond is possible where one party seeks to impose his will. So it is that husbands surrender the love of their wives and wives the love of their husbands, so, too, parents sacrifice the devotion of their children when they seek to mould them to their own subjective plan. They may succeed in making children obedient, respectful, servile but this is not the mutual love on which lasting happiness is built. Only selfish social friendships are built on bribes. The moment I start to use a friendship for my own private profit, pleasure or amusement, the personal bond is snapped. How many homes fall apart for this. No human being likes to feel that his friendship is being used. Here lies the rub in business, sex, family life, sport, entertainment, politics. The alternative to using my friends for my own convenience and promotion is to love my neighbour as myself.

Professor Macmurray, who writes with so much wisdom and feeling on this complex subject, describes our genuine, personal relations most beautifully. I need make no excuse for quoting him again. He writes:

> Now, contrast this with a personal relationship or association, a friendship for example, between two men or two women. If the two people are associated merely for what they can get out of one another it obviously is not a friendship. Two people are friends because they love one another. That is all you can say about it. If the relationship had any other reason for it we would say that one or other of them was pretending friendship from an ulterior motive. This means in effect that friendship is a type of relationship into which people enter as

persons with the whole of themselves. To ask David what he expects to get out of his friendship with Jonathan is to insult him by suggesting that he only associates with his friend from self-interest. No doubt he might answer that he gets everything that makes life worth living; but of course what he means is that he gets friendship out of it, which is exactly what he puts into it. This is the characteristic of personal relationships. They have no ulterior motive. They are not based on particular interests. They do not serve partial and limited ends. Their value lies entirely in themselves and for the same reason transcends all other values. And it is because they are relations of persons as persons. They are the means of living a personal life.

Now we understand what the personal life is in distinction both from the individual and the social life. It is the life which we live as persons, and we can live it only by entering into relationships with other people on a fully personal basis, in which we give ourselves to one another; or, to put the same thing the other way round, in which we accept one another freely for what we are, and in which therefore there is and can be no purpose other than the sharing of our lives in fellowship. The impulse to do this is simply the impulse to be ourselves completely; not to gain anything, not to achieve anything, or to do anything in particular, but simply to be ourselves as fully and completely as is possible. Now we have only to state this and grasp it to realize that the whole significance of human life is to be found here. What other significance can our existence have than to be ourselves fully and completely? Obviously none. In the nature of things this must include in some way everything else. The social life and the individual life can only be subordinate to this. They are necessary as a basis for this. In other words the whole network of organized human association has only one meaning; that it is the necessary foundation on which the personal life can be built. Society exists for the life of personal relationship. Personal life does not exist for society. To think it does is to try to stand the world on its head . . . this enables us to see at least what the personal life demands. It demands a relationship with one another in which we can be our whole selves and have complete freedom to express everything that makes us what we are.

Clearly I am hoping that you will derive so much encouragement from these admirable paragraphs that you will not charge me with labouring the point. Though obvious, it is missed by so many people who do not see personal relations as "the whole significance of human life". And yet, if we call memory into play and gaze back over the incidents of a long lifetime, we may ourselves prove the Professor's point.

In a previous chapter, I compared our unconscious mental background to the index of a book. Given a subject on which the Ego requires information, consciousness consults the index and twenty, eighty or two hundred memories are speedily evoked. Throw up a word like 'toothache', as I have said, and one may re-taste buckets of mouthwash and re-smell the cloves. Take the word 'holiday' and back come the jumbled memories to haunt you, anything from ice-cream at Clacton, to the sea off Sennen or live lobsters in the market at Bordeaux. So clear are many of the pictures that one may even look an imaginary sea-gull in the eye.

As we have been thinking of personal relations, let us propose the word 'friendship' and ask the memory to consult its dossier. Hardly have we formed the word than a flood of memories overwhelm the conscious mind. Heart and mind dart up and down and sideways as words, gestures, letters, snapshots, scenery, partings, silences, tears and laughter flash before our inward eye. For some, sadly enough, the word evokes scarcely a tremor; for most of us, the exercise is both poignant and breath-taking and brings a lump the size of a life-time to the throat.

I am hoping that you will find, as I do, that such memories of friendship are not concerned with trivial incidents. Rather, they produce, in the very innermost recesses of our being, a deep, lasting and wellnigh un-bearable ache. Here, in the centre of our hearts, is the very essence of personal love. For, just as the adver-tisers on TV· show us whole fruit being squeezed and concentrated into a single fruit drop, so experience has concentrated the love of a lifetime into an essence strong enough to bring tears to the eyes. Incidents may have been forgotten or discarded but the memory of deep affection still remains. Say the two syllables of Mother or Father and, maybe, the affection of thirty years is back with us again. So with the love of hus-band and wife, the infant devotion of one's children, the deep understanding of friends not seen for many years. Even where a marriage has failed or a friendship has been shattered, those first untainted moments of personal love are still preserved. Time seems to heal all scars, remorse makes a painful reparation and all that was genuine in the friendship still survives. To return to the one safe imaginative illustration, the leaves and the stalk and the blossom may wither but the fruit of friendship remains.

Have you noticed this further point? In more distant

days we may not have been so clear, but when we re-call the memories of friendship, the genuine friend-ships, and these only, return to the mind. Other liaisons, alliances, companionships have not survived. At the time they seemed to enjoy all the outward marks of friendship, the confidence, gifts, endearments, promises which time has now exposed as sham. They may have been emotionally more intense but they were person-ally less honest and they now remain, if they remain at all, under a less complimentary head.

On the other hand, true friendships, even of short duration, still survive. Friendships cannot be measured in units of time. A sudden and fleeting acquaintance-ship may seal a friendship which dwells in the memory for good. These genuine ties were based on freedom, mutual sympathy and understanding, an ability on the part of each to be himself. There may have been in them few promises, no presents, not a trace of sex. They occur between people of different age, different nationality and colour, different religious outlook, diff-erent political beliefs. They survive to colour the scenery; to enhance the splendour of the greatest poetry shared together, to erase the sorrows of a life-time and to foster hope. When such a friendship is killed by death, the mourner lacks the courage to view again the favourite towns and trees and buildings through sad and tearful eyes. Fra Angelico himself seems to lose something of his colour if I last went to Florence with a now departed friend. And have you noticed that such friendships are, often, timeless? Death may end the contract but the essence of that personal understanding survives.

One cannot escape the sentimental overtones when

writing of such friendships, but the fact of them is coldly based. The joy of life has, in fact, been the joy of friendship for our whole machinery was designed for this. There may have been other pleasures in life but, on examination, we find that most of them were tied to friendship in some particular way. So the study of a certain subject, appreciation of art, the passing of an examination, a rise in pay, a civic honour, are now for ever associated with the encouragement and spontaneous pleasure of a friend. Yes, there have been considerable pleasures in life, at table, in books, through art, by industry and perseverance, but the foundation of human solace has been human fellowship.

Maybe you have noticed, too, in such human relations, a strange, deep, unexplainable conviction that such unions will never end? The personal bond seems to survive the grave. Here is a fact so profound and so persistent that we dare not brush it aside and remain true to ourselves. Call it wishful thinking, explain it as the quaint survival from a more primitive tradition, deny, if you wish, the chances of any personal survival and yet, in the lowest or highest reaches of our being, the conviction of personal reunion remains. To try to picture it would be to picture nonsense, to ignore it would be to dodge one of the most extraordinary facts of life. I would go so far as to say not only that we will one day be reunited to parents, wife and children but that, though they are dead, we are in union with them now. If you have never become aware of this, simply say that I am wrong. The yearning for friends in the centre of the heart is neither morbid nor mournful; it may have been sharp at the time of their death but this bitter pain soon passes; the yearning for them grows more intense, more young, more hopeful as the years pass. If you cannot agree with this, you may be one with me in this assertion that personal friendships are the salt of human life.[2]

SYMPATHY

These long-drawn considerations bring us back in the closing stages of the chapter to our thoughts about charity. The traditional view of charity as the stooping down to help the less successful may easily lead to patronage. Who would want to deny the excellence of generosity in all its forms? It is, however, one thing to praise philanthropy and another to accept it as the sole or supreme expression of human fellowship. A careful analysis of worthwhile friendships, the nostalgic memories of mutual understanding, show how little friendship relies on financial aid, influence, preferential treatment or bonuses. Our dearest friends may never have been called to offer us a helping hand. They gave us gifts which were far more lasting, understanding and sympathy.

Sympathy has been defined as the spontaneous reaction to another's joys and sorrows and, as such, it may be the highest form of personal charity. For sympathy is based on an awareness of other people, an appreciation of their nature, their rights, their liberty, their aspirations, virtue and dignity. Sympathy is spontaneous, not studied, springing as it does from sensitivity. It embraces the rich as well as the poor, the fortunate as much as the unfortunate, because it is the spontaneous reaction to the joys and sorrows of our fellow men. Consideration of past friendships helps to underline this point. The deep conviction that true friendships cannot die is explained by the awareness in our mental background that we have been both understood and loved. In vain we try to picture the dead, for imagination fails to recreate them while old albums only present their features at a certain age and date. The essence of their friendship is still savoured and it is the essence of sympathy.

Sympathy enjoys certain peculiar characteristics which make it seem much more easy of attainment than the traditional charity. It hinges more on awareness than on love. While it often remains very hard to feel any love for one's neighbour, it is not so hard to be aware of him. Again, as has been said, the word 'love' has now acquired so many connotations that we are not very certain what kind of love our neighbour ought to have. Some try so hard to pretend this love that they switch on a charitable expression which gives them facial paralysis and their neighbour a pain in the neck. Sympathy demands no such contortions, it begins with an awareness which leads us to get to know our fellow men.

Awareness of other people and a modest effort to get to know them invariably put us in their debt. Where the traditional charity works the other way round to the embarrassment of the donor, an interest in others produces no such patronizing effect. We ourselves gain by such interest. Poor old Scrooge was grateful to the boys. How often when we take children out for the day or escort foreign visitors round our city, we end up as debtors because of the interest and kindness they conveyed. Sympathy for others in joy and sorrow is the most satisfying experience known to man. Grasping this truth ourselves and tasting its delights, we become aware of the need to grant a similar interest to others that they, too, may attain the same happiness. To keep myself to myself may be a subtle, cruel way of forcing others into loneliness. Put the other way round, we begin to see that mutual awareness leads to knowledge, mutual knowledge to sympathy and mutual sympathy in our day-to-day behaviour is translated by such traditional words as friendship, love and charity.

It would be wrong to suggest that human sympathy is equivalent to supernatural charity in its most profound Christian form. Sympathy in itself is not supernatural and all of us for purely natural motives feel sympathetic towards many of our friends. Sympathy and antipathies may be based on purely natural traits. At the same time it may be fairly argued that sensitive awareness leads to unselfishness. We react spontaneously to the joys and sorrows of others and thus begin to find our true objective happiness outside ourselves. Let us regard sympathy as the first, faint but sure sign of that charity which, in Christ's words, leads to a man laying down his life for his friends. I doubt very much if anyone could have supernatural charity without sympathy but one could have sympathy which failed to develop and remained purely on the natural plane. I have stressed sympathy here rather than charity to avoid those overtones and undertones which surround and obscure the word 'charity' today. Sympathy may be easily recognized and the motive which leads us to react spontaneously to the joys and sorrows of other people may deepen to true charity if we let grace have its way.

My own views of this quality were greatly modified after an extraordinary lecture given by a middle-aged Polish priest. This good man, arrested at the age of eighteen, spent six years in Nazi concentration camps. His sentiments were scriptural. He was not a priest at the time but became one after the war. In his lecture, after recalling the cruelty, the hunger, disease, the lack of hope, the sight of suffering all around him, he outlined the conclusions to which his long imprisonment had led. He recalled how he had been compelled from sheer necessity to forgive his enemies if only to preserve his sanity. So many of his fellow prisoners drove themselves mad with hate. He saw that Christ was speaking from a deep understanding of human nature, that forgiveness, even in the face of so much injustice, was the prerequisite for peace and happiness.

Next, he found that some of the Nazi guards, even those whose cruelty was proverbial, responded to kindness and, surprisingly, showed on occasion an unexpected tenderness. One of the worst of the guards eventually took a liking to him because he reminded the poor man of his only boy, killed at Stalingrad. The Polish lecturer also learned in Belsen that education, culture, gentle birth were no guarantee of honesty. Faced with starvation, many an educated prisoner was driven to implement the meagre rations at the cost of his fellow prisoners. Who would blame men in such a state? Yet the Pole found that in such a crisis, many coarse and criminal types with doubtful records proved that they loved their neighbour as themselves.

My Polish friend at the close of his lecture spoke with considerable feeling, asserting that he had experienced in Belsen a happiness which he had sought in vain ever since. Said he simply, "I was dying of dysentery and two fellow prisoners nursed me, saving their own pitiable rations to build up my strength. I had no possible way of repaying them, indeed I was expecting to die before morning, yet I had a glimpse of untold happiness at being loved simply for myself."[3]

The testimony of this simple priest—those with similar experience have since confirmed his verdict— brings us to the bewildering implications of this virtue taught by Christ. Pictures of Christ rarely do credit to his manhood; not the gospels but the artists made him a pale Galilean and charity a sad and anaemic exercise. Yet careful attention to the Gospel text is rewarding, demanding as it will a shift of emphasis.

This is no Scripture text-book; I must make my points briefly and move swiftly on. First, one is surprised by Christ's seeming preoccupation with this virtue so that as much and more space is given by him to our relations with our fellow human beings as he devotes to our relationship with God. Page after page, line by line, he deals in detail with our approach to others, passing from the sublime sacrifice of life for other people to the more trivial tendency to jostle each other in the queue. His teaching culminates in the Our Father and one is forced to the conclusion that he found it easier to show men the meaning of a heavenly Father than to explain the plural form of the personal adjective.

Next, while there can be no doubt at all about Christ's deep concern for the poor, the sick, the helpless, his attitude to charity went so very much deeper than health or cash. Almsgiving as such had its place and its importance but to him it was only one manifestation of charity. The corporal works of mercy were part of his life and part of his teaching without in any way exhausting his teaching on relationships. One should record as a corrective that Christ himself had many rich friends. He was, in fact, classless, and his teaching on charity was neither Tory nor trade unionist. Nothing is clearer than his rejection of righteousness or of patronage. The widow who gave her mite was picked out from all the benefactors to the Temple, to pass into history.

Perhaps our interest is aroused more by his own example of awareness, showing itself in sympathy. He was aware of the old lady who touched the hem of his garment, of the embarrassment of the newly-weds at Cana, of the fear of Nicodemus, of the hunger of Jairus' little daughter, of the plight of Malchus who had lost an ear. He noticed the little Zacheus up a sycamore tree. Nathanael was astonished that Christ had noticed him. He knew that the twelve had been arguing on their journey, that Peter was keeping back the children, that the two disciples journeying to Emmaus were sick at heart. He not only suffered with the sick but he rejoiced with the disciples on their mission, asked the Samaritan woman to give him a drink of water and so made it easy for her to confess her sins. In the same way, he allowed a prostitute to dry his feet with her hair though he knew very well what his enemies would say. So he sat down to a meal with Levi and a group of publicans. I am, myself, always astonished at his awareness of others during the last agonizing hours of his life. He remembered to glance at the penitent Peter, to cure the miserable Malchus, to heed and reward, in his own agony, the courage of the thief. More astonishing still, he reacted spontaneously to the predicament of Pilate and excused the behaviour of the Roman Governor at the very moment of his cowardice. He even showed sympathy for Judas and advised him to complete his treachery at once. At Gadara, he showed both sympathy and insight for the devils in their homelessness.

Perhaps the most powerful lesson which we learn from Christ in his personal relationships is the liberty which he allowed to those whom he met. Following our definition, he consciously adjusted his behaviour to the nature of those outside himself. He forced no one, left each free to respond or not as he wished. Peter, John and Andrew were free to follow him or not and to call their own friends. Judas was not prevented from stealing or from going to the priests. Though he told Pilate that he had no power, he allowed the Governor to exercise power at his expense. In the parable, the guests who decided to dodge the banquet were permitted this discourtesy. "He who has ears to hear, let him hear," he said to the crowd on one occasion, the only attitude even for God in such a personal approach.

For Christ makes it very clear and he alone was in a position to do so, that the God who created us accepts and maintains this personal relationship. God, unimaginable, a spirit, neither male nor female, is yet a person and as such gladly accepts our personal liberty. As Zacheus, according to St Luke, "stood upright before the Lord" though he was short of stature, so we, though pigmies, stand upright before the Lord of Hosts. Here is the significance of Christ's whole approach and the poignancy of those particular parables in which he shows God reacting to our personal prerogatives as though he were one of ourselves. The story of the

Prodigal is the supreme example of this fact. Christ made the same lesson very clear on many other occasions, explaining the behaviour of God by what we ourselves would do in a like situation; "If anyone of you owns a hundred sheep and has lost one of them, does he not leave the other ninety-nine in the wilderness and go after the one that he has lost until he finds it?" The forgiveness of the unworthy son may be the most poignant feature of the parable but the true lesson lies in the implication addressed to human persons, "Would you not do the same yourselves?"

So long a chapter, based on friendship, written round the theme of true personal relations, has carried us from the loneliness of our bedrooms almost to the throne of God. The self-knowledge which we set out to find in the opening chapter ends in self-forgetfulness. Yet we cannot forget ourselves just by wishing to. How many people, in trying to forget themselves, think of themselves the more. The only way in which I may learn to forget myself is by learning to acquire an alternative and more attractive interest.

It would be pleasing to assert that the love of God himself is so all-absorbing that in it we may forget ourselves. We may rarely count on this. St Francis de Sales wisely reminds us that, of all human emotions, the love of God comes last. Theologically God comes first and my neighbour second; psychologically, my neighbour is the first, the stronger, the more immediate attraction, and through my awareness of him I come to the supreme awareness of the personal God.

Two Apostles stand as witnesses to this. St John, who was at the foot of the cross and who knew more than any man of the love of Christ and of his mother, makes that astonishing pronouncement which should have us praying and puzzling for years. Writes John: "If you love not your neighbour whom you see, how can you love God whom you do not see?" I used to think that one first loved God and next, for his sake, with much puffing and blowing, accepted a bunch of not very appetizing neighbours as well. In theory this may be, partially, correct. In practice, however, the approach will be very different, for the greater our interest in and awareness of our neighbour, the more we may grasp God's awareness of and interest in ourselves. The power of God is seen in the physical laws which bind all creatures, the genius of God is mirrored in the skill and intuition of the artists, but the love of God is glimpsed only by those who have experienced the love and sympathy of their fellow men. If we make the love of our neighbour the guarantee and measure of our heaven, we will be keeping our lives close to the Gospel text.

So it was left to St Paul to write the most exquisite passage ever penned on this fundamental virtue, a passage which starts in heaven with the tongues of angels to drop to the banalities of everyday life. Paul writes of patience, kindness, tolerance. Was he speaking of the love of God? He was and yet he had no option but was forced to measure our love of God by our personal attitude to men. When he had established this—and only then—was he able to soar again into the heavens, using of our relationship with God the very language which Professor Macmurray employed to describe the love of human friends.

There is ecstasy in Paul's inspired lines but only for those who so love their neighbour that they are able to guess the type of love of which the Apostle speaks.

Says Paul: "We see now as in a mirror darkly, but, then, face to face. Then I will know even as I am known."

"To know, even as I am known" is the final promise, the definition of a personal friendship in this world and in the next.

I

6

NO FEAR

IF, as I believe, awareness of God's love for us is acquired through this sympathy for our neighbours, then, at some stage of our investigations, we need to sit down to examine our consciences carefully. St Ignatius of Loyola, middle-aged and, at the time, a wounded soldier, spent more than a week over this exercise. He was not so much searching for sins as for a sense of shame and confusion; he was also examining his conscience to test his motives and to compile his future pattern of life. Our need may be similar to his. For so many of us, it is not only sin that needs uprooting; we must also tackle a crop of worries and a harvest of self-seeding fears.

FEARS

I have yet to meet a Christian who is free of fear. This is hardly surprising for the fear of God is the beginning of wisdom and, though Christ our Lord said, "Fear not" on many occasions, he also said of God the Father, "Him you must fear indeed". Our task must be to distinguish between the fears which are irrational and pointless and that basic acceptance of God's authority on which our very happiness will be built.

The first of the irrational fears concerns our own examination of conscience, for we are well aware of its inadequacy. In middle age we know the difficulties and now know, at least in secret, that we will never reform ourselves. We gaze back with envy to those younger days in which we could form sweeping resolutions which seemed to work. It is not so simple now. In middle age we have the parable of the Cockle to guide us, for in tearing up the evil we may loosen our virtues as well. On the other hand, we are frightened to do nothing, for to leave well alone is to leave ill alone, with disastrous results. In the end we decide to do nothing, but such inactivity only makes us fuss. Five years ago, in Canada, I heard a salutary story of an alcoholic who went on pilgrimage to a famous shrine to seek a cure. He prayed to Our Lady and was cured. Said a friend of his: "Yes, his prayer was answered and he has not touched a drop since that day. The only trouble in his case is that he has now substituted a far worse habit instead." There is much wisdom in this tale.

Are we growing lax? If we take ourselves as we are, we naturally start to worry for we all have a tangle of bad habits and unworthy motives in our lives. It is from the heart's overflow that the mouth speaks and if our hearts have for years been manufacturing self-love, self-interest, self-pity, the resulting self-centredness will have permeated our every gesture and every act. While in middle age we all wish that we were better, we are also aware of our annual deterioration and decline. Which of us has not noticed in ourselves a general coarsening in the question of sex? Drink, which once we watched so anxiously as an insidious habit, has now joined forces with our bread and butter to become one of the necessities of life. The right pattern of daily prayer to which for so many years we remained faithful is now shattered, and we know ourselves to be too restless and distracted to resume such a burden again. Our very faith seems to be both stronger and weaker for, while we could not live without it, we cannot persuade ourselves to give it the importance it deserves. An atmosphere of mild depression obscures the conscience and many of us experience that odd sensation of judging and acting in a dream. Easier, perhaps, to cope with one or two high calibre offences than with this decay of spiritual morale. Said a friend to me, "My conscience is so jaded," or, as another put it, "I cannot take a serious situation seriously."

Now I would not want to over-paint the picture and each must judge for himself how far my outline fits his facts. Those not so jaded are better off and should cling with vigour to their freshness, cutting these pages and the author's middle-aged melancholy. Those who share with me this sense of failure may, at least, sing with King David to the God who gave joy to our youth. Be very certain that there is joy in middle age, a joy far greater than we ever had in childhood but far more subtle, a joy which is only attained when we are free of fear. For, like the dead Romans of Virgil's day, *live* Christians have to pass their Cerberus. Theirs is a seven-headed fear. Fear that we are humbugs, that we have forgotten our past sins, fear that God will prove harder than we think, fear that our standards are too low, that we will never put things right, that we will be unprepared at death, fear that God will disown us for eternity. These are the sources of our terror, the breeding-ground of tension, the obstacle to that eternal happiness whose radiance, even in this world, should touch and colour our lives.

If we want to be rational and consciously wish to

adjust our behaviour to the nature of the world outside us, then we should concentrate our whole attention on the only fear that matters, the salutary and rejuvenating fear of God. So many of our other fears are entirely imaginary and may safely be discarded to afford us the time for the one exercise which is objectively sure. We must persuade ourselves that life would not be worth living without a salutary fear of God. The alternative to such a fear is utterly repulsive, for a God who could not command our fear would be no God at all. In a book which is but an introduction to an introduction, one cannot treat a problem as deep as fear exhaustively. The most that may be achieved is an exhortation to set aside all fears which are based on past and future for such fears are concerned with facts which cannot be altered or with imaginings which may never see the light of day. I cannot change the past however much I worry about it, nor can I foretell the future with certainty. Fears based on past or future are not only foolish but also damaging. They distract my attention from the present moment in which the fear of God leads to contrition, love and happiness.

As we have already seen, a sensitive awareness of the world outside us implies a sensitive awareness of Nature's inexorable laws. No creature has even been able to escape them and true satisfaction is found in facing this fact. Thus only do we arrive at humility. Half the humbug and restlessness of our social life springs from a culpable blindness for we behave like those, mentioned by St James, who, after looking at themselves in the mirror, go away and forget what manner of men they are. See those self-important men and women, their living bodies already a prey to maggots, who yet dress up and preen themselves in public and strut about so pompously. The politician with the greatest following in the morning could be on the coroner's slab in the afternoon. Lord Mayors with chains, society dames with flower-pot hats, tycoons with seven figures to their bank balance cannot for all their gargling fight a winning battle against a determined germ. Let us be very certain about this. Our insecurity from day to day deserves continual attention; those who try to forget it suffer fear and strain and tension, those who face it enjoy both humour and happiness. No matter what we do, no matter whether we are dowsed with holy water or soused with Gordon's, we must pass from this life at the appointed day. When people now talk about the happiness and heroism of the London blitz, a period free of self-importance and class distinctions, they forget that this atmosphere of fellowship was created in the objective humility of a possible sudden death. Death is as near today and those who accept the fact live honestly.

Total acceptance of this utter dependence on God is the raw material from which we manufacture humility. The lie that caused the fall of man, "No, you shall not die", still deludes and deceives men today. Though one never meets a man silly enough to deny that he will die some day, one meets thousands who dismiss the subject, saying to themselves, "I will die one day but not just yet". Just as soon as we can persuade ourselves of the present emergency of our existence, the fear of God becomes a live and salutary fact. In the present moment, God may do with me as he wills. I cannot picture him, I gain nothing by imagining the day of judgment but I stake a claim to sanity if I take my pulse. God is no further from me than that. It need not surprise us that so humorous a man as St Thomas More, peaceful, tolerant and witty, wrote a vivid book on the fact of death at the height of his brilliant career.

Moses fell flat on his face before the Lord and the same gesture of submission, suitably adapted both to country and to climate, must be made in Brooklyn, Sydney and Shepherd's Bush. Marcus Aurelius, the good pagan, went as far as he could when he welcomed to himself the inevitable laws of nature; the Carthusians on their mountain, high above Grenoble, do it better, singing the *Gloria Patri* with head and shoulders bowed. Here is the one genuine, rational fear worth enduring and worrying about. Middle-aged we may be, varicose-veined and jaded as to conscience, but each year better equipped to make this act of humility. The young may have their noble ideals and sweeping resolutions; we have a far more vivid aid to holiness in the fact of death.

I stress this point so strongly in order to underline that most useful corollary which springs from this central fact. The fear of God is best expressed and best accepted in the manner in which we apply the laws of nature to ourselves. Stones and sparrows have no option but we, as human beings, may willingly and cheerfully embrace our state. No need to worry about the past or to fear the future if, in the present, we live by faith. For death itself is the punishment for sin and we best show our sorrow not by worry but by acceptance of the sentence passed on us. We may show God by our behaviour that we think his judgment just. Nor need we fear laxness in the glad acceptance of daily aches and pains.

Guilt melts away, remorse is removed, anxieties

lifted, when, instead of saying that I am sorry, I show my sorry by the way I bear my life. Hurrah for rheumatism, gumboils and bad nights! All human beings suffer such trials and all possess the power to convert such troubles into a solid act of faith. As an old lady once said to me, "I cannot now pray as well as I used to but, you see, I have my rheumatism instead". In place of her rheumatism you and I may have to substitute nerves, loneliness, a broken home, hearing aids, loss of health, cash or reputation for we all have more than sufficient raw material for the making of a life-size saint. Pain itself comes from without to both Christian and agnostic; it is refined and fashioned into Christian acquiescence in the centre of the heart.

The advantage of seizing the chances which God provides lies in the escape from wishful thinking, so damaging a practice in the spiritual life. We cannot fool ourselves about physical distress. Nor can we fool God who has bound all men by the laws of nature and knows his friends by the way in which they trust in his providence. In every sphere of life, it is always so much more simple and so much more holy to cling to objective fact.

THE TYRANNY OF THE SHOULD[1]

Unfortunately, most of us are not prepared to face the facts. Instead of showing both our sorrow and our faith in the tangible ways which God has provided, we like to find even our worries in an imaginary world. So we remain vaguely apprehensive about our faults and about our conscience and this very anxiety is in great part imaginary.

Much of the dissatisfaction which we now endure,

so many of the harsh judgments which we pass on ourselves and others, spring from the urge, already mentioned, to actualize our idealized selves. What began in
early life as unconscious imitation has ended in dis-
illusion because we have not become all that we
imagined we could be. We need to go back to the
Gospel story to restore our sanity.

'The Tyranny of the Should' has this in common
with all other forms of dictatorship that it invariably
leads to duplicity. Recall if you will the political dicta-
torships of Hitler, Mussolini and Stalin under which all
citizens had to appear in public loyal and law-abiding
while the black market, smuggling, secret plots and
printing presses flourished underground. When such a
tyranny is centred in the human imagination, the same
public observance will conceal the same secret deceit.
The Tyranny of the Should with its arbitrary laws about
what one should be able to do, its fury with self in the
face of failure, is every bit as crazy as any other dicta-
torial regime. It commands the same lip-service, the
same play-acting, the same duplicity. The personal
tragedy is possibly worse when tyranny resides in the
imagination, for few will be brave enough to admit such
deception in themselves. Unless we are strong enough
to challenge our own false standards, even our own
high standards when these are falsely founded, we will
continue to live fraudulently. It is for this reason that
one nurses a secret sympathy even for the Pharisees.
Many of us without intention have fallen for the very
faults which were theirs. We may easily form too dark
a picture of the faults of ourselves and others unless
we grasp that our very standards are based on a false,
subjective pride. Worse still, we may waste many years

of our lives in attempting a type of perfection to which God never designed us and which is, in fact, unattainable.

I pass by the Tyranny of the Should, as it is manifest in so many secular occupations, for we should by now be able to recognize the snobbishness which worldly fashions impose. Part of our present sense of failure derives from a worldly judgment as to what is meant by success. Do you remember being told that it was cowardly to cry, that a gentleman should never show his feelings, that success, money, status, the keeping up with the revolting Joneses was a 'Must' in life. Hence, even in our everyday lives, this tyranny forces us to 'keep up appearances'. We talk about books which we have never read, we repeat filthy jokes because these are thought to be manly, we sow our wild oats as the price demanded for maintaining a place in a social clique. The Tyranny of the Should, which finally toppled Pontius Pilate, will lead in our lives to the same conventional cowardice.

Here, the spiritual plane is more important and the tyranny much more difficult to trace. Christ himself put before us a series of spiritual standards and these obviously we should obey. The Church which exercises his authority continues to place the Christian rule of behaviour before men and women of each succeeding age. Where an unbeliever may, if he wishes, shake himself free of all restrictions, Christians have a code of behaviour which they freely wish to obey. The Tyranny of the Should does not apply to the commandments for the commandments are no tyranny at all. They are objective and are so designed and fitted to man's nature that they offer happiness. The Christian laws of behaviour are so simple and so satisfying that those who obey them escape fear and anxiety for good.

Yet imagination remains imagination even on the spiritual level and it always tends to avoid the commandments to present an idealized form of holiness which Christ never taught. Our *oughts* and our *shoulds* seek to make us more Christian than Christ, more Catholic than the Pope. With them goes the poisonous presumption that God will gladly give us grace to attain these false ideals. We come to presume that he wants us to be what we imagine to be best. Bound hand and foot to such false spiritual ideals, no longer can we move. Our spirituality ceases to be outward-looking and is wholly concerned with our imaginary states. We feel vaguely sinful, always apprehensive, constantly depressed. We complain that our prayers are never answered, that we get no better, that all our efforts are to no avail. All the time we are striving to actualize our idealized selves. God does not answer our prayers because, though we do not grasp it, we are turning ourselves into Pharisees.

St Paul hints at all this in a very famous passage in his second letter to the Corinthians in which he at least makes clear to us that God had a very different outlook from his own. You will recall that the Apostle suffered from some grave trouble which seemed to be damaging his life. The experts differ in their comments, some think that his sting of the flesh was a temptation to lust, others judge that it was a physical weakness, others, that his previous behaviour drew to him so much opposition that he was impeded in his apostolic work. St Paul himself tells the story very simply in these words: "And indeed, for fear that these surpassing revelations should make me proud, I was given a sting to distress my outward nature, an angel of Satan sent to rebuff me. Three times it made me entreat the Lord to rid me of it; but he told me, My grace is enough for thee; my strength finds its full scope in thy weakness. More than ever, then, I delight to boast of the weaknesses that humiliate me, so that the strength of Christ may enshrine itself in me."

Just as soon as we are strong enough to boast of the weaknesses that humiliate us will we put an end to the spiritual Tyranny of the Should. For the fact is clear that we are not strong or capable of much virtue and we were wrong in youth when we thought that we were. Our dissatisfaction with ourselves in middle age may be more a sign of progress than we guess.

It will, however, take many years of humble practice before we will be prepared to boast of our weakness with St Paul. Unlike the great Apostle, we have our idealized image of holiness, partly of our own invention, partly fobbed off on us by our parents, by devoted friends, priests and teachers who themselves were reared on that imaginative diet served up in so many biographies of saints. The lives of the saints become dangerous for those who want to romanticize themselves. Once a false picture of holiness has been formed in us, a perverted generosity drives us forward as we struggle pathetically to make such an idealized picture come true. Too late we discover that the saints were not as we supposed them to be. So determined are we to succeed that no amount of warning will make us change. That Augustine was for many years impure, Peter cowardly, Jerome ill-tempered, Becket ambitious, Ignatius scrupulous, Philip Neri eccentric cannot now alter our impression, our certain failure, our bitter sense of remorse.

The tragedy of this Tyranny of the Should in religious matters lies in the fact that its dictates are clearly based on what is good. In our long list of grievances against ourselves and others, a very great number of our desired practices are, in themselves, excellent. So we say, "If I really love God as I *should*, I *should* be able to kneel down for my prayers, I *should* give up drink, I *should* cut out smoking. I *should* go to Mass daily, I *should* eat less and I *should* read better books". Our reasoning continues in the approved scholastic form, "but I do not kneel for my prayers, give up drink, cut out smoking, go to daily Mass, eat less or improve my reading, therefore I do not love God". To make matters worse, we then think of other holy people, past and present, who achieved these very standards in which we are failing and their very example serves as salt to rub into our sore but very egocentric wounds. St Teresa knelt for hours at a stretch, Fr O'Flaherty has taken the pledge, my father gave up smoking, Mrs Ponsonby goes to daily Mass, Mrs Carey reads St John of the Cross in Spanish, so where will I be at the judgment day? Comparing ourselves with others is always a symptom of this tyranny.

The curious feature of such recriminations is that they deal with subjects not remotely concerned with sin. No commandment compels me to kneel for my prayers, to give up drink, to cut down smoking, to read St John of the Cross in Spanish or to make myself like Mrs Ponsonby, Fr O'Flaherty or any other of God's saints.

"Ah yes," we reply, "but we feel that we should."

Here is the Tyranny of the Should in its most vicious and most subtle form. It disguises itself cleverly as a feeling and we never pause to ask ourselves whether it is an honest, rational feeling or not. How very different is our attitude from the candour of St Augustine who, after writing pages about his troubles against purity, ends with the glorious sentence, "It is with no doubtful knowledge, Lord, but with utter certainty that I love You."

THE PHARISEES

This Tyranny of the Should is seen in all its horror when we consider where it leads. It turns men into Pharisees. Seeing the humbug in ourselves, we must surely feel compassion for those scribes and elders in the Gospel who stood so near and yet so far from holiness. Set out elaborately on paper, their spiritual practices would have challenged the achievements of the greatest saints. The Pharisee praying in the Temple told no lie when he boasted that he was not as other men. He fasted, he prayed, he kept the Sabbath, served in the Temple, avoided impurity, observed all the ritual washings and yet lacked that vital quality which could have made his prayer acceptable to God. Little did he know, for this book had not then been published, that he was trying to actualize his idealized self. His was an imaginary holiness which God could not recognize. His effort did not spring from the overflow of the heart. He was an actor and played on the public stage the part of a saint. He was duly applauded for it and found his credit before the eyes of men.

To achieve his standard, he was certainly hard on himself. In secret, in his bedroom, he would have compared himself to others, as in fact, he was doing in his prayer. How much we must be on our guard about this. Such a comparison would either have fanned his complacency or driven him to futher effort in a frantic attempt to keep up with the best. All his fasts, his prayers, his austerities were unconsciously designed for this. William Law, the Anglican writer, describes the outlook of this Pharisee and of all who are like him, so very well:

> Hence we may learn the reason why many people not only lose the benefits but are even worse for all their mortifications. It is because they mistake the nature and worth of them. They practise them for their own sakes, as things good in themselves; they think them to be real parts of holiness, and so rest in them and look no further, but grow full of self-esteem and self-admiration for their progress in them. This makes them self-sufficient, morose, severe judges of all those who fall short of their mortifications. And thus their self-denials do only that for them which indulgences do for other people; they withstand and hinder the operation of God upon their souls and instead of really being self-denials, they strengthen and keep up the Kingdom of self.

The full tragedy of the Pharisees has this added poignancy that they wanted in a twisted, self-centred way to be good men. Yet, when Christ moved among them curing the sick, consoling the poor, encouraging sinners, revealing the mysteries of God's kingdom, they, the officially holy people, were no longer able to recognize objective holiness. On the first Good Friday evening, after they had killed him, they possibly went to the Temple, probably thanked God that they were not sinners like that Jesus Christ.

This gigantic hypocrisy, based on false evidence brewed in the imagination, must stand as a grim warning to us all. Given false, imaginary standards, duplicity will always be the fruit. How far we are culpable in this one cannot say, and we may hope that God will make allowances for the silly habit of self-glorification formed unwittingly in youth. Though we may be forgiven, our self-sown suffering and disappointment may be very great.

Duplicity is a painful spiritual disease. We say one thing in public, think another in private and live in terror of giving ourselves away. We are compelled in public to play our part, to impose burdens on ourselves and others, which, secretly, we know very well we will never observe. After a time our fear of death and judgment turns less on the anger of God than on the anguish of having our duplicity revealed before our friends.

Or again, have you ever noticed, as you look back from middle age, that past confessions seem much less reassuring, less because we have deliberately omitted a sin or have lacked contrition, more because our very examination of conscience has been hypocritical? We wonder how far we limited our past confessions to the subjective trivialities of our idealized lives.

I sometimes picture a Gospel Pharisee going to confession for he, too, would have had very few peccadilloes to confess. He might have accused himself of carelessness in the Sabbath law, he might have had distractions in prayer or missed an occasional ritual washing, he may even have given bad example by speaking to unworthy people, such people as sinners and Samaritans. Certainly he would have accused himself of negligence in fasting and of not reading the Torah with care. How different his verdict of himself from the verdict of history about him and his caste.

To recover our balance on this question of sin, we must return again and again to the objectivity of the Gospel story for Christ never permitted any imaginary idealization of ourselves. No scruple of any kind has Gospel backing and those who strain over a gnat and swallow a camel will have little encouragement from him. Examinations of conscience based on the Gospel precepts would prove extraordinarily helpful and refreshing, providing us with matter which would busy us for years.

As we might expect, Christ would turn our attention away from distractions in prayer, gluttony, impure thoughts, cursing and swearing to our treatment of our neighbour, from which so many of our faults have originated, on which our love of God depends. Do not take me up wrongly, for obvious sins on these and others subjects must be duly considered and confessed. Yet the fact remains that so many of our troubles and anxieties today spring from the ease with which in the past we have made a bee-line for the doubtful, semi-conventional transgressions and have dodged the true issues which the Gospel story underlines. If only the Pharisees had turned their mind for a moment from these endless ritual washings and Sabbath-day observance, they might now be sitting with the saints. They failed where Magdalen, Zacheus, Matthew, Peter and Paul, who were honest sinners, were given grace enough to change their lives. The Pharisees did not want to change their lives.

K

MY ATTITUDE TO MY NEIGHBOUR

In the first place, we must reassure ourselves that there will be no possible laxness in focusing our whole attention on one particular sin. As the love of God is our one desire, we must seek it where it may be most easily found. As sins of uncharity obscure the vision of God so swiftly, these we must tackle first. The love of God, when found, proves so all-pervading that it will spread to every level of our lives. If I grow in personal love of my neighbour, I will, without doubt, also grow in patience, tolerance, purity. My charity will change entirely the colour and content of my prayer. In my confessions, let me say my piece and seek forgiveness, but when I examine my conscience I would do well to attend, mainly, to charity. Christians of all ages and sizes suffer from scruples but few of these are ever concerned with charity.

Secondly, I must make it clear to myself that I myself will be the gainer, for, as we have seen, my attitude to my neighbour will decide my capacity for loving God. In a lonely, self-centred heart, there is a lonely, self-centred God. Writes St Francis de Sales: "The measure of our love for the Divine Goodness of our Father in heaven rests on the perfection of our love for our brethren and companions on earth." Put the other way round, offences against my human brethren limit my ability to love God. If you do not love your neighbour whom you see, how can you love God whom you do not see?

Thirdly, we should rejoice that Christ, by placing so much emphasis on the practical side of this fundamental virtue, has provided us with an easy escape from the subjective world. Nervous breakdowns will be far fewer if and when we love our neighbour as ourselves. Further, he it will be who will have the breakdown, from surprise. We need so much to adjust our consciences in middle age. We cannot afford to upset ourselves with fears, panics, guilt complexes and scruples, but all these subjective terrors melt in the presence of objective charity. I must risk being taken wrongly to remind you that the man who loses his life will find it and that charity such as this causes us to worry about our own personal salvation less and less. I am not saying and do not mean that a reader who has committed murder may forget about it on the plea that he is concentrating on charity. I do mean, however, that we may forget the past entirely and the seven-headed fear already mentioned, to base our lives entirely on the Gospel count.

There need be hardly any doubt about the arrangement of our programme, for Christ entered into the smallest detail and has almost left us with a syllabus. The correction of humbug becomes for us not a matter of pious aspirations or of wishful thinking but a practical exercise.

First, take the Gospel story and see how Pharisees were formed. Their first recorded symptom is that they "murmured in their hearts". From this they passed to forming a distinction between the more and the less worthy of their neighbours, after that, they showed a preference for a code of law against a love of people, finally they came to accuse others of being less devout, less austere, less holy than themselves.

I cannot tell you how to stop murmuring in the heart about your neighbours but those who succeed in conquering such a universal practice will qualify under the beatitude and will see God. This inner criticism of others is the start of hypocrisy.

Christ himself provides a very simple and concrete cure for humbug, not to impose on others burdens which we are not willing to carry ourselves. His long and biting attack on the Pharisees continually returns to this. Before we begin to consider how to love our neighbours, we must watch to see how we treat them in this very practical way. The Pharisees imposed such burdens, financial, legal, intellectual, ritualistic, based on an inner conviction of their own superiority. They said in effect, "This is what we, the holy ones, manage to do". Such an attitude deserves careful attention even today.

Parents impose burdens on their children, husbands on wives, schoolmasters on boys, priests on parishioners, patients on doctors, employers on workmen, travellers on hotel servants, which they would reasonably resent and refuse to do themselves. Clearly I am not thinking of services freely undertaken for a just wage. A master in school is hardly expected to undertake every English exercise which he sets for his class. But should he demand respect, civility, prompt obedience, punctuality when he himself attempts none of these courtesies when he is dealing with the staff? How often we expect from others cheerfulness, punctuality, efficiency, tidiness and the mastery of moods. We feel that they should answer our letters by return. We demand of a fellow citizen not to park his car in such a way that we cannot get to ours. Put the other way round, we ask for ourselves a certain dignity, the right to our own opinion, a modicum of leisure, our fair share of consideration, approval and applause. Sincerity comes into sight for each of us when we adopt a single standard of judgment for our neighbours and for ourselves.

The genius of Christ is seen in the simplicity of the famous question which he put first to the Pharisees and puts to all of us. "How is it that thou canst see the speck of dust in thy brother's eye and art not aware of the beam which is in thy own?"[2] You notice that even in sin we are back to "awareness" again. Somehow we have to find an answer to this question and an honest examination of conscience must concern itself with that.

THE SPECK IN MY BROTHER'S EYE

Much thought is needed before you and I can see the full implication of this question to which Christ invites us to reply. In the end, I think that we are forced to the painful conclusion that we see the speck in our brother's eye because we are looking for it and want to find it there. The process of condemning others works out rather in this way.

You and I and our fellow men are only able to reach each other by the use of external signs. However much we may sympathize with each other we cannot, in fact, speak without gestures, signs, language, never heart to heart or soul to soul. If it is from the overflow of the heart that the mouth speaks, then all our words, gestures, facial expressions, intonations are the means whereby our personal aspirations are conveyed to the world outside ourselves. We have no other means of communication but these. Even our dress, our taste, our gait, our carriage are conscious or unconscious channels for our personality. Sadly enough, in all our efforts to communicate with others, there is an oft-repeated note of appeal. We not only want to reach other people but we want them to respond. We all desperately desire that others will approve of us.

Now, when we seek to make contact with other people, we are all of us liable to be misunderstood. This happens in three ways. Our words are open to several interpretations and may be misunderstood. Our intonation, inflexions, gestures, facial expressions may convey very different impressions and alter the meaning of our words. Lastly, our very appeal to our neighbour may be taken in a variety of ways. How often it happens that three or more participants in a conversation take three or more different impressions away. Indeed to hear two accounts of the same conversation is, often enough, to listen to two completely different tales.

Outside the theorems of Euclid, every communication between persons is open to misinterpretation and an uncharitable person deliberately places the worst possible interpretation on his neighbour's words, gestures and appeal. Why? There is no other possible answer to the question but the true one, that, secretly, he dislikes his neighbour and derives some perverted pleasure in seeing him fail. Just as a pessimist truly enjoys bad news and will read all the signs awry to get it, so an unsympathetic person really wants to see the speck in his brother's eye. He, naturally, would never say so, even to himself. His unkind reaction may be unconscious but, nevertheless, it is from the overflow of the heart that the mouth speaks. His heart is sour and he takes his neighbour's words and appeal in the least kindly sense. When dealing with himself he allows himself the benefit of every doubt. When dealing with his neighbours, he grants no such benefit.

Cardinal Newman remarks that men entertain prejudice only against their fellow human beings and that they cling to prejudices, not because they believe them to be truthful, but rather because they do not want to surrender them. If they dislike another, they are delighted to accept any unkind rumour and to presume it accurate. Their enemy is guilty until such time as he may prove his innocence. Says Newman rightly, "To resolve that rumours and suspicions shall be true is simple malevolence. deplorable, shocking, inexcusable."[3]

Now Christ never asked us to go through life with our eyes tightly shut. I am not required to ignore my neighbour's errors or to walk about with a fatuous grin of universal fellowship on my silly face. There would be humbug in such make-believe. Not only do I see my neighbour's faults but I am allowed by Christ to judge them, for his words "by their fruits you shall know them" imply a reasonable judgment on my part. How great the difference between such an objective judgment and that bitter interpretation of the smallest peccadillo, stemming from pride and prejudice.

Christ himself suffered from just this. The Pharisees misinterpreted the tears of the sinful woman at the supper, the action of the disciples walking through the cornfields, Christ's visit to Zacheus, his meal with Matthew and his cure of the blind man. A different interpretation was possible on each of these occasions— each alternative proved to be the right one—but the

Pharisees did not want the truth. Despite their broad phylacteries, their fasting, their loyalty to the law of Moses, they did not love their neighbour as themselves. Indeed, they thought as badly of their neighbour as they possibly could. Christ's answer to them is frightening in the context; "Do not judge others or you yourselves will be judged. As you have judged so will you be judged, by the same rule; award shall be made to you as you have made award, in the same measure." When we examine our consciences, here is the subject to be considered first.

In his instructions on our examination of conscience Christ seems to focus our whole attention on the treatment of our neighbour and to avoid all subjective imagery. His first rule is clear enough and I will repeat it, that we must not impose burdens on others which we are not prepared to shoulder ourselves. There can be no honest scruple, doubt or misunderstanding about this. Next, he invites us to take always the most sympathetic interpretation of our neighbour's action as he himself will do for ours. It is this approach which will lead us to forgive injuries, to turn the other cheek, to show mercy, to get out of bed in the middle of the night when our neighbour knocks.

Where we may worry ourselves sick about the guilt of past sins, about loss of faith or middle-aged laxness, there is no room for worry or misunderstanding in Christ's laws of charity. We need no expert advice to inform and direct us, for we know very well the burdens which we impose on other people and the kind of interpretation we give to their acts. We have only to consider carefully the reasons why we dislike certain people to discover the precise grounds on which our less charitable interpretations are based. If what our neighbour does is objectively bad, then it is reasonable to condemn it as Christ himself condemned the behaviour of the Pharisees. Should it, however, come to light that our antipathies stem from a subjective motive, at least we will know what to confess and what to guard against. Most antipathies arise because the other party lacks respect, ignores my rights, is insensitive about my feelings, makes demands which I feel to be impertinent, or in some way or other challenges my security.

SINS AGAINST SYMPATHY

In a previous chapter we were considering our personal approach to others, beginning with a sensitive awareness and moving towards sympathy. We noted that the satisfaction of such friendships as we form lies in the fact that neither party has an ulterior motive and that both friends may freely be themselves. Such friendships are not founded on convention, need no protocol, pretence or gamesmanship. We also saw that such human sympathy and understanding is the prerequisite for any approach to God. For all these reasons, especially the last, it is essential that we should remove all possible obstacles to charity. If the vision of God, as I firmly believe, will turn on my love for my neighbour, then I would be very foolish in middle age to worry about any other point than this.

We make no mistake when, in middle age, we let drop every other anxiety of conscience to concentrate most fully on that field of faults which may do most damage to the soul. Let us worry about impure thoughts, distractions in prayer, cursing and swearing after we have given our neighbour his due. Christ said very little about distractions in prayer, impure thoughts or Sunday observance and though this does not imply that such subjects lack importance, it may suggest a reassessment of our priorities. The Tyranny of the Should may safely be limited to charity.

St Paul, in the famous passage already quoted, heavily underlines this lesson taught by Christ. The Apostle starts with the astonishing statement that learning, faith, martyrdom, prophecy and miracles come a poor second to charity. He does not stop at this but makes it clear that he is speaking of personal relations for he adds the remarkable statement, "I may give away all that I have to feed the poor but if I lack charity it goes for nothing". Such a remark must come as a shock to those of us who have worked on the false assumption that giving alms is of the essence of charity.

From such sublime and sweeping thoughts, Paul suddenly drops down to the sad, trivial, dull, little details to those small, intimate, domestic decisions on which happiness in Cleveland, Ohio, Hampstead, Hull and San Francisco finally must rest. He speaks of practices immediately applicable in convents, presbyteries, homes, offices, hospitals and schools. Strange that our heaven should turn on little points like these. Why do we not put our prayerbooks away with their long, exhaustive schemes for examination of conscience, with their sins of idolatry, superstition, graven images, charms, omens, sacrilege and blasphemy? The confessor might receive a shock—for all we know he might himself be led to follow our example—if we made our weekly confession from the headings given by St Paul. Then, at last, we would be knocking down the barriers which shut us in and make us subjective and block for us the vision of God. Says Paul, "Charity is patient, is kind; charity feels no envy; charity is never perverse or proud [perversity looks very much like sulking], never insolent; does not claim its rights, cannot be provoked, does not brood over an injury; takes no pleasure in wrong-doing, but rejoices at the victory of truth; sustains, believes, hopes, endures, to the last."

You may have noticed in this passage that if you substitute the word "Christ" for "charity", you have the perfect epitome of the life of Christ on earth.

One last significant fact. For those who make small effort in the field of human charity, the figure of Christ, majestic and historic, remains curiously aloof. Always sympathetic, he yet appears distant and austere. As soon as we begin to try to love our neighbour, our relationship with Christ himself undergoes a very subtle change. He becomes more alive, and we begin to see him as the unifying spirit of the Scriptures, bringing a heterogeneous group together and holding them together by his love. All the ingredients of a personal relationship are present in his dealing with each one. We begin to see Peter, Magdalen, John, Nathanael, Nicodemus bound together in personal friendship because they each loved the same, extraordinary friend. Christ allowed to each the dignity of a human person, he finding his happiness in them and they in him. Each one of them was free. They had their rights, their views, their initiative, their responsibility. Christ gave to many of them nicknames, an unusual and unexpected trait in God. Something in him kept this first band of disciples together, uniting them, not only to each other, but to

Abraham and Moses and, down the ages, to people like ourselves.

One notices in the lives of so many saints this same growth of Christian friendship and awareness stemming from Christian charity. So Paul was utterly changed outside Damascus not only in his relations with other people but in his personal friendship with the Jesus whom unconsciously he had been persecuting through his friends. Augustine sheds his self-centred learning and conceit, and his love for his mother Monica grows more and more tender as he grows more and more aware of Christ. In our lives we, too, will be able to probe the mystery of Christ's charity. "No man comes to the Father but through me," he said to the disciples, and it would seem, in practice, that no man comes to Christ without charity. It is hard to distinguish cause and effect, to know which comes first, to identify the action of grace in such personal relations, but the mark of love is always present in an awareness of the world outside ourselves, an awareness of our neighbour, an awareness of Christ as an historic figure, an awareness of a deep and personal friendship with him, finally, the sudden awareness of what it means that he is the Son of God.

7

THE LAKE IS RISING THROUGH THE GRASS

NEARLY fifty years ago, when I was very small, my parents took us to the country to stay with distant cousins on a large Devonshire estate. Far more attractive to us than the house itself, for all its beauty, were the many mysteries of a nearby lake. So, after lunch one day, while our elders were enjoying both their gossip and their coffee, we children set off without permission to explore the fringes of this pool. An iron lever on the very brink proved an immediate attraction and we, laughingly, joined forces to heave it forwards and backwards many times. Soon the game palled. We were back on the lawn with our fond Mammas when an ancient aunt exclaimed in her refined, unhurried manner, "Mary, my dear, are you aware that we are drowning? The lake is rising through the grass."

This use of the word 'aware' when a lake was bubbling up around us has remained to amuse me for many a day. The incident, too, may serve as an apt example of the action of grace in the spiritual life. Certainly, St Teresa chose a similar comparison when she sought to describe the various forms of prayer. She pointed to the different methods of watering a garden; the more laborious operation with buckets and a windlass and the easier way "by a stream or brook which waters the ground much better, for it saturates it thoroughly and there is less need to water it often, so the gardener's labour is much less." The psalmist, too, picks a similar simile when he sees the just man standing "as firm as a tree planted by running water, ready to yield its fruit when the season comes".

The theme of this book is, probably, helped by my aunt's prim exclamation, "Mary, my dear, are you aware that we are drowning? The lake is rising through the grass." At least it underlines the need of awareness, for the action of grace is silent and underground. We see nothing and hear nothing but, as we gaze above and direct our prayers towards heaven, we are nourished through our roots. We may feel no better but, unconsciously, we may begin to behave much better; we love ourselves no less but love God and our neighbour more. Christ's parable of the seed that grows secretly is verified in us. We become aware that the plant is growing though we never see it move.

Awareness, as I have tried to show in these pages, is a vital spiritual attitude. As the little girl in the telephone booth gradually grew aware of the world outside her; as the traveller made himself aware of the city in which he was sojourning; as the young Pole became aware of human friendship in the despondency of Belsen, so are we suddenly aware of God. In this the personal pronouns have their importance, for when You and I are fully aware of one another, we also become aware that the very bond between us is the third personal pronoun singular, spelt with a capital.

Awareness, then, must be our part of this personal friendship whose growth is a gift from God. To follow this growth, let us, in this final chapter, consider the astonishing development which we ought to find in our middle-aged prayer.

Prayer by definition is the raising up of the mind and heart to God. Who raises up his mind and heart? The answer must be 'a person', and how very important it is not to overlook this essential point. We must ever be aware in prayer that we are persons with our personal dignity, liberty, initiative and responsibility. Though God made us out of nothing, he, of his love, decided to make us personal human beings, not cabbages or sheep. Just as the prodigal son was interrupted by his father when he tried to assume the part of a servant, so we cannot gain God's attention unless we pray as our own inimitable selves. It is the mark of personal friendship that each friend should be himself. Each must be entirely at home. Whatever method of prayer we decide to use, we must make very certain that it does not kill that which is personal and spontaneous. God does not want from me long extracts from a prayer written by St Alphonsus unless this good saint happens to have said, and said better than I can, all that I long to express.

There are prayerbooks galore and methods galore, for every holy writer as a person developed in his day a personal approach. I, too, must exercise my personal liberty in this, picking and choosing, for any method is good which aids me in raising up my mind and heart to God. I may improvise or borrow, for in prayer there is no copyright. I may pray in church, in the fields, on a bus, in the bathroom; pray on my knees or sitting or standing, pray silently or by reading, speaking, humming, whistling, so long as my choice of method raises my mind and heart to God. On paper there may seem to be a risk of irreverence, but rarely in practice; all true personal friendships are based on reverence. Job

certainly spoke his mind to God. The little Zacheus
stood upright and Paul could write to Timothy with
bewildering assurance, "He to whom I have given my
confidence is no stranger to me and I am fully persuaded that he has the means to keep my pledge safe
until the day comes".

LITURGICAL PRAYER

In prayer we must go our way, for we are persons
and should freely accept our responsibility. Yet human
nature is the same in its aspirations and limitations, and
our love for God and for our neighbour may best be
expressed in conformity. Whatever our social differences or personal quirks, we human beings share a
common nature and may come together as actors on
our public level to act in unison our submission to
God.

One of the very first signs of true spiritual progress
in us will be an awareness of the charity of the liturgy.
By nature, and when in public, we are actors and the
liturgy is a dramatic presentation of our love and common homage, played on a public stage. So the hermits
of ancient Egypt left their solitude and desert hide-outs
to come together for this public act. Where a liturgy is
dead, neither our love nor homage will be worthily expressed. Just as drama, ballet, opera, suffer peaks and
troughs across the centuries, so the effectiveness of the
liturgy may fluctuate century by century. When the
Second Vatican Council discussed liturgy first, this was
not to suggest that it was an easy or unimportant subject but rather a gesture of recognition that here was
one of the most powerful spiritual influences in life.

A long disquisition would be unfitting here and the liturgy is mentioned for the part which it must play in our awareness and, hence, in our personal attitude to prayer. Its glory should entrance us and its measurements amaze us, dramatizing as it does the history of man since Adam's day. It speaks to God and to men of all ages and all nations by means of every art, blending painting, literature and music in the setting of the greatest architecture and with the aid of every human craft. How many of the most inspired works of human genius from our own day back to the splendour of the great Greek Temples were created in the service of man's liturgy.

As with charity, you will find that the liturgy takes on an entirely new meaning as soon as you grasp that it is not optional. Misunderstandings over so many years, the gradual sapping of liturgical vitality, have led so many of us to adopt an artificial attitude. The strange division between so-called liturgical and popular devotions has introduced a spiritual class-distinction into the very act of homage which we pay to God. Again, note the confusion between the liturgical and the monastic which has led many to identify the liturgy with cowls, tonsures, gothic architecture and Gregorian chant. Intelligent people are led by this to draw up an unreal list of personal priorities: "I am for Catholic Action, you are liturgical, he, poor fellow, is only devotional." Yet more absurd is the expression which I myself have often heard from those who should know better, "I dislike the liturgy, it disturbs me at my prayers".

As our liturgy is, at the moment, in a state of transformation, the mistaken enthusiasm of individuals may have fashioned prejudice and provided certain grounds

L

for complaint. Yet the fact is clear enough that when we go to church for a public service we would be silly to expect much chance for private prayer. Surely there is a note of contradiction in the very notion of gathering in public for private prayer. How unreasonable it would be if a visitor to the theatre in Stratford-upon-Avon complained that the actors disturbed him in his reading of Shakespeare's script.

Private prayer, as Christ clearly indicated, must be made in our inner chamber with the door firmly closed. We come together in public to participate in a drama, to express through our presence and by the use of signs and gestures all the love that has overflowed from a full heart. By attempting private prayer in public, we impose on ourselves a wellnigh unbearable strain. We are for ever struggling with distractions which we deliberately invited in the very act of coming to church. Of course I will have distractions if the toddler in the bench ahead deftly lassoes my glasses with her father's rosary beads. No use whatever blaming myself, blaming the babe, blaming her father, God the Father or Fr O'Flaherty, the parish priest.

The strain which comes from attempting one form of prayer in a place designed for another is not only frustrating; it also robs us of the relief which the liturgy is designed to provide. As human beings we earnestly need the opportunity to show our common awareness and sympathy for others by forgetting ourselves. Private prayer in public destroys this community spirit and makes us 'separate'. This very separation in turn makes us critical. Before we know where we are, we have started to resent our neighbour's presence, to dislike the priest, the altar boys, the choir, to sign our-

selves devoutly while picking mental holes in our neighbour's hat. We are back in the Pharisees' boat. they
reading the Bible, we with our *Key of Heaven* in our
sanctimonious hands.

My ordination to the priesthood taught me a salutary
lesson and showed me how far our modern liturgy may
have failed. I discovered that a priest at the altar is
unable to say any private prayers. Sentiments, impressions, desires pass through his head as he recites the
official words and performs the gestures assigned to
him. He cannot pray privately as some of the congregation feel that they should. The plight of a bishop is
more extreme, swathed as he is in many vestments and
with a mitre on his head. He may not be able to recite
private prayers but he certainly prays. His presence is
a prayer. Altar servers recite few prayers while the
choir can hardly manage one Hail Mary with mouth
wide open, one eye on the baton and the other on the
score.

When first ordained, a young priest may feel mis-
givings about this sudden change of emphasis. I recall
various efforts to squeeze in a few reflections, for these,
I thought, and thought wrongly, were essential in every
form of prayer. Such efforts have long since ceased.
Most priests move through Mass with spiritual awareness to take the place of private thought. We lend our
presence, our voice, our lives that the gestures may be
accomplished and the deed done. The liturgy is a public
prayer by signs, culminating in the glorious moment
when Christ comes sacramentally to make with us and
for us his sign of the cross.

From the liturgy, so understood, we may all derive
a new and lasting satisfaction, substituting for our

private devotions an awareness of God and of our
fellow men. A glorious collection of personal pronouns
go flying through the air. These should be more than
enough. True charity is shown in this sacrifice of our
own subjective moods and fancies and in the fellowship that others in the congregation offer us in return.
I find as a priest that the profound bow which I make
when reciting the *Confiteor* is by itself as complete an
act of sorrow as are the words. How the contrition of
the congregation would be enhanced if the people, too,
could only stand and bow. Perhaps soon they will. The
only obstacle to prevent them is the very unspiritual
yardstick that such things are never done.

Liturgical prayer in our public lives is an essential
for those who have grasped the message of this book.
We are by nature actors and the Church in her wisdom
caters for our need. She provides the stage and script
and costumes for our act of faith. Actors, once the
curtain is up, forget themselves. So, too, should we.
Our moods, despondencies, scruples, fears, distractions
make little difference so long as we have enough control to play our part. Years ago, the father of a very
famous London actress dropped dead on Christmas day.
Not to disappoint the crowds, she, despite her sorrow,
heroically appeared for the Bank Holiday matineé. In
just the same way, we sink our private joys and
sorrows to unite with the Church in a common act of
prayer.

In middle age we may well find an increasing joy in
this liturgical awareness which takes the strain from
our feeble and weary brains. The Church does the
thinking for us and we pipe up to say Amen. Christ
himself makes the act of obedience for us while our

agreement is signalled by our presence in the church. Sometimes Mass passes like a dream. I used to think that this was very slack and very sinful, that I must rouse myself to rattle off petitions from a book. Now I am not so sure. Sleep during Mass or deliberate laziness would be disrespectful, but a certain type of spiritual awareness, as the mystics tell us, appears to be very much like sleep. One may be present at Mass and apparently doing nothing while, spiritually, fully aware of all that is being done. As with the woman already quoted, one may assist at Mass as one may listen to music with the soles of one's feet. The raising up of the mind and heart to God is our one consideration and this we may do with or without a prayerbook, with or without feelings, with or without thoughts.

One further liturgical thought. Only three days ago, a letter reached me from an Englishwoman, back in London after fifteen years abroad. For eight consecutive weeks she has attended daily Mass in a London parish without a word of greeting from a single soul. Each member of this congregation certainly carries to Mass a private batch of worries along with his or her missal or rosary beads. Yet the liturgy of this parish fails to link common charity with the common act of sacrifice. The people receive communion at a common rail, are in communion with each other without feeling any desire to communicate. The liturgy must forge a bond of sympathy between us or London will share the unenviable lot of that other holy city whose liturgy began and ended with rubrics and a series of empty rites.

Liturgical prayer is not confined to the high-altar Masses of a Sunday but must exercise its benign control over every department of our public life. The duty of acting reasonably, of adjusting our behaviour to the nature of the world outside us, becomes very much more easy when our public prayer is adjusted first. If we do not pray properly in public, we cannot expect to live properly. I may kneel for hours at a stretch in tense, subjective, imaginative prayer of petition, but if I get up at the end more touchy, more self-pitying, more ill-tempered, then it may be that I should change my method and be humble enough to unite in prayer with my fellow men in church. If I identify myself with my fellow men, reciting the same words, bowing my head with them in sorrow and acceptance, I at least avoid the danger of becoming a spiritual snob.

As it is from the heart's overflow that the mouth speaks, no liturgical exercise will be personally effective unless it is inspired and motivated by the aspirations fashioned in our private rooms. Humbug is the besetting threat for actors and for liturgists. Caiphas swung as pretty a thurible as any prelate and bowed as low as any priest. Had that other Pharisee of the Gospel story prayed in St Kentigern's instead of in the Temple, his prayer, though liturgical, would not have been more pleasing to God. Maybe he would have been thanking God that he was not as the rest of the congregation, unliturgical Irish folk who knew no better than to rattle their beads during Mass. As the said unliturgical Irish folk might also have been thanking the Mother of God that they were not snobs like the English liturgists, God would be placed in the delicate position of deciding which of these prayers he disliked the more. The moral for us must be that it is very, very dangerous to start thanking God that one is not like other people, while the solution to the problem is to start praying in one's room.

PRAYER IN PRIVATE

Christ told us explicitly, when condemning ostentatious prayer, that we must pray in private, and I will quote his words in full: "But when thou art praying, go into thy inner room and shut the door on thyself, and so pray to thy Father in secret; and then thy Father who sees what is done in secret, will reward thee."[1] The liturgy pleases God always because it is the whole Church with Christ at its head which employs it, but God's attitude to my personal share in the public words and gestures will be decided by what he sees me doing in my room.

The expression "Go into thy inner room" is but a metaphor for privacy. St Thomas More, when he had become Lord Chancellor of England, was able to afford a private oratory in his Chelsea home.[2] Some distance from the house he erected what the family used to call 'the new building', to which he retired every Friday for the day. Not all of us will be as fortunate as the great Lord Chancellor, living as we must in cramped conditions and rarely alone for ten minutes in the day. Yet Christ's insistence on privacy must, somehow, be met if ever we hope to pray.

Masters of the spiritual life, among them St Francis of Assisi and St Bernard, had acquired after years of practice the ability to recollect themselves anywhere. Francis Xavier would pray all night while tramping across the Japanese hills. St Teresa tells us that this ability to pray privately in public comes only to those who are far advanced in holiness. For most of us privacy is essential, and only a deep-grained humbug allows us to dispense with it. That, at least, is my experience. We must, then, find or make some privacy at any cost. In the Middle Ages, when everyone lived in a central hall for the sake of the heating, the mystics could only find privacy by making for the woods. Where, pray, in our days, may most of us find woods? We must procure our privacy in an empty church when the public services are over, on a country walk, in a churchyard, even in a car. A car has enormous potentialities so long as one leaves the radio alone. Or it may well be that, from time to time, we must miss a family outing, a sacrifice worth making for privacy. We cannot survive without it and there is something strangely disturbing about a Christian world which has hardly noticed its loss.

Certain clear rules must govern our behaviour in our rooms. To take the negative aspects first, we must, at whatever cost, avoid that imaginative mooning which is purely selfish and which stimulates the unhealthy desire to idealize ourselves. Such an imaginative surrender to subjective success, to self-pity, remorse, grievances and indignation must be ruthlessly denied. There will never be an escape through the imagination; those who try it will, sooner or later, be forced to slink back to their telephone booth again. Freed of such self-centred thoughts, imagination may well become a great spiritual blessing, reminding us of God's mercies and of the love of our friends.

Next, when we are alone, and after we have curtailed our imaginative mooning, we must make the effort to face ourselves. Carefully considered, such a routine acceptance of ourselves as we are today, with all our weaknesses, failures and frustrations, is a living act of faith. It is a prayer in itself. Many who find it difficult to pray for long, whose nerves and fears and scruples play havoc with more formal acts of devotion, may yet attain to the heights of prayer through the courage with which they face themselves. For some it will be loneliness, for others the dread of ill-health, for many the sense of purposelessness and the fear of not being wanted, for all the knowledge of failure, which will raise the mind and heart to God. People say to me, "I find that I can no longer say my prayers", not fully grasping that "Waltzing Matilda" sung badly in the bathroom by an over-fifty may carry as much courage and conviction as the Nicene Creed. I knew an old priest who took up painting as a hobby; he painted very badly at all hours of the day. He said to me, "My painting may be poor but it is better than self-pity; if I can avoid that, I may leave the rest of my life in God's hands".

If, in our inner rooms, we are able to face ourselves and to cut out all imaginary mooning, then our Father, who sees what is done in secret, will reward our courage and our love.

One further important deduction stems from this basic attitude. Some devout souls are afraid to make use of the ordinary relaxations to lessen the pain of loneliness. They fear that they will become lax if they enjoy themselves too much. To seek distraction and entertainment seems to them unworthy when they should be fixing their hearts and minds on higher ends. It is my experience that God directs each one differently but always towards that pattern of behaviour which will make us more and more ourselves. It is of the very essence of personal friendship that each friend should be himself. On the other hand, the Tyranny of the Should is viciously active even in our bedrooms, seeking always to make us act artificially. How great the difference between "I long to love God better" and "To be really holy, I should be able to do this".

The legitimate use of relaxations—theatre, movies, novels, sport, music, television—should be considered with care. On this subject St John of the Cross supplies a good example which may serve very usefully in middle age. He takes the case of a small boy who has picked up a carving knife. A wise mother does not attempt to snatch it from him but she distracts his attention with a more attractive present offered to his other hand. Unable to think of two things at once and drawn by the prospect of a new acquisition, the little boy grabs the other present and, unconsciously, releases his hold of the knife. God seems to work in this way with bad habits, and when it comes to legitimate relaxations we should allow him time to offer us something more rewarding in their place. Until he makes a move, as he always does, we should be prepared to use all lawful forms of relaxation, for charity towards our neighbour demands that we should be no more crazy than we have to be. The two most secure guides in the matter of relaxation will be the Liturgical Calendar with its feasts and fast days and the general progress of our prayer.

The true solution to this question of self-denial and legitimate relaxation will be found in the pattern of our lives. A sane programme of prayer will tend to produce a sane man. In theory, I can think of God and pray to God at any moment of the day or night. Psychologically and in practice I have to exercise prudence for my soul may not be wired for too great a load. Attempt too much too quickly and a fuse will blow. If, as a reasonable human being, I must adjust my behaviour to the objective world outside me, then I must begin by adjusting my spiritual exercises to my own capacity. To be myself, I must maintain a balance in my public, private and inner lives. Too much liturgy in public and I may end up with Caiphas, too much meditation without some liturgical expression and I may grow melancholy and morose. Little by little, God will show me how to fix the proportions; as it costs very little after the age of forty to survive without toffees, so it will be easy to abandon TV and paperbacks when the time is ripe.

In considering our private lives, we have noted the danger of imaginative mooning and the need to face up to ourselves. We saw that "Waltzing Matilda" hummed in the bathroom might, in a moment of panic, serve as a very fair substitute for a formal act of faith. The sparrows in the Gospel story probably chirruped; why not and still more, we? Up to this point our thoughts have been turned to remote preparation, for we can hardly hope to pray as Christians unless we behave as Christians in our inner rooms. That intimacy with God in prayer which we may now examine runs parallel to this spontaneous confidence.

MEDITATION IN OUR ROOMS

There are methods in plenty to pick from when we come to meditation and each of us should feel free to suit himself. The saints wrote about prayer with so much first-hand experience to draw on that we may well want to follow their advice. Whether we apply our imagination to the Gospel scenes or argue with ourselves about deep spiritual problems, we must start by raising our minds to God. "No one can love what he does not know" and the first requirement for true spiritual progress is to increase our knowledge of God.

For myself, and taking into consideration the conditions in which so many of us are living, I would put spiritual reading first. Here is the easiest and most rewarding form of meditation, exactly suited to our modern requirements. Others may prefer the precise rules for meditation laid down by the great spiritual masters and, on so intimate a subject, each of us must choose for himself. One should not ignore the fact that conditions of life have altered considerably since St Ignatius' and St Teresa's day. Further, so many of the acknowledged masters were catering for the needs of a specialized group. St Ignatius drew up his spiritual exercises chiefly for those who were withdrawing from their daily occupations to make a long retreat. Francis de Sales wrote for men and women of leisure, Teresa for contemplative nuns. The rules which they suggest are of universal application only if allowance is made for the altered situation in which we find ourselves. Some of us have no time, others no privacy, others insufficient knowledge, most of us too much tension and very little peace. The situation in modern Balham differs very greatly from that of seventeenth-century Annecy. Spiritual reading is of equal importance in every century and in every country for, without it, we have little chance of knowing God. Nor is this a revolutionary suggestion, based as it is on the practice of all the saints and especially on the example of the Fathers, whose intimate knowledge of the Scriptures has fashioned the thought of all Christian people across the centuries.

It may well be that the traditional method of meditation by the application of Memory, Understanding and Will will fit more easily to our modern conditions if we expand it to cover the whole day. So we apply our memory through the liturgy of daily Mass with its selected passages from Scripture, our understanding during spiritual reading, and our wills in that inner prayer of the heart which we must consider next. No fault can be found with those who raise their minds and hearts to God at different times and in different ways. It is pleasing to note that the author of *The Cloud of Unknowing*, basing his advice on well-established medieval practice, offers to one whom he calls "a contemplative prentice" the three headings, Reading, Thinking, Praying.

Meditative reading becomes so very much more easy when we persuade ourselves that we can have no valid excuse for omitting it. We can never reach God and it would be impudent to expect to, if we make no real effort to think of him. Spontaneous and original thought may be far too hard for 'rush hour' commuters but any fool with sufficient good will should be able to read. Many of us, however busy we are, find time for the morning and evening papers, a couple of glossies and heaven knows how many columns of small ads. We are humbugs if, for all our protestations of affection, we cannot be bothered to read about God for months at a stretch. I become more and more aware in middle age that thoughtful reading is the surest and safest test of sincerity. We may read a little every day or, following the example of St Thomas More, a man

as busy as we are, set aside one full day in every week.
There should be one day in every week in which we
miss TV and all social engagements, saying truthfully
to enquirers, "Sorry, I have a previous engagement",
an engagement which we all owe to God. Here, in-
cidentally, was the purpose of the Sabbath but in the
twentieth century God would not be fussy if we prefer
to set aside another day.

It would be out of place to consider the content of
our reading here. Sufficient to underline that this type
of spiritual reading is undertaken mainly to stimulate
our sensitive awareness, not to cram our minds with less
important facts. Many books officially catalogued as
spiritual will raise neither the mind nor the heart to God.
If we are searching for sensitive awareness, the Sacred
Scriptures stand supreme. It is hard to believe that anyone will attain to genuine holiness without a deep love
and appreciation of these. Nor is it possible to read the
Scriptures slowly without achieving that sense of personal attraction which is for most of us the prelude to
prayer. Beyond the Scriptures, we may select from
whole libraries of books, some officially spiritual, some
labelled secular but both capable of raising the mind
and heart to God. To read Dom Bede Griffiths' *The
Golden String* is to see how Shakespeare, Shelley, Dante,
Plato led one pilgrim upwards towards God.[3]

THE PRAYER OF OUR INNER LIVES

In our second chapter we set out the three layers of
existence and now, at the end of the book, we seek to
suit each layer with its own special form of prayer. In
actual life the divisions may seem less neat. Sufficient

if we recognize that, in the main, liturgical prayer will best suit our public homage, spiritual reading, our efforts to raise our minds to God in our private lives. We cannot, at least, deceive ourselves if we are faithful in these. However slack we may feel, however weary, we need hardly doubt our progress if we are constant here.

As it is from the heart's overflow that the mouth speaks, that the body acts, that love towards God and man must be exercised, much turns on the quality of our prayer in our inner lives. Geographically, we are still in our inner rooms with the door shut. Our private and inner lives are both simultaneous and parallel, they fuse with one another from time to time. The aspirations of the heart come into action without warning and cease as suddenly. A striking feature in the life of St Teresa is the suddenness with which she was carried away. For her and for other great masters of prayer, this union with God became almost continual, whereas for most of us the divine intimacy will occur swiftly and in spasms, divided from each other by minutes, hours, months, or even years.

To describe this prayer of the heart, I would like to use two long quotations, taken from the writings of two very extraordinary men. These passages will serve as an introduction, tracing the gentle way in which the private life with all its confidence, fears, bliss, tension and loneliness, merges with the interior form of prayer.

Now Thomas More, a lawyer, twice married, once Lord Chancellor of England, built himself, as I have already said, a private oratory. Every Friday he retired there. Not even his eldest daughter, the beloved Meg, knew his secret and we may only guess at it today. Yet,

later in his life, sitting in the Tower of London await-
ing execution, More wrote a book for the consolation
of his family. Three-quarters of this book is concerned
with a commentary on the Scriptures, especially on
those psalms which had comforted him. But, of a sudden, he sets out a description which seems to reveal the
secrets of his private oratory. The whole passage would
prove far too long but the opening paragraph shows, in
very simple language, how one very holy layman
started his approach to God.

> Let him also choose himself some secret solitary place
> in his own house as far from noise and company as he
> conveniently can, and thither let him sometimes secretly
> resort alone, imagining himself as one going out of the
> world even straight into the giving up his reckoning unto
> God of his sinful living. Then let him there before an
> altar or some pitiful image of Christ's bitter Passion (the
> beholding whereof may put him in remembrance of the
> thing and move him to devout compassion) kneel down
> or fall prostrate as at the feet of Almighty God, verily
> believing Him to be there invisibly present, as without
> any doubt He is. There let him open his heart to God and
> confess his faults such as he can call to mind, and pray
> God for forgiveness. Let him call to remembrance the
> benefits that God hath given to him, either in general
> among other men or privately to himself and give Him
> humble hearty thanks therefor.

Thus wrote the Lord Chancellor at the very end of
his life and just before his execution and we cannot
doubt that he here reveals the source of his courage, his
humour and his peace.

At the very time when Thomas More was Chancellor,
a Spanish student came from Paris University to London

to beg for alms to maintain himself. He was a middle-
aged man, an old soldier, later to become famous as
the founder of the Jesuits and as an expert on prayer.
Ignatius of Loyola, after his sudden conversion, spent
a year as a hermit in a remote Catalonian cave. Here he
practised all those many spiritual exercises which,
later, he was to set down in his celebrated book. As his
methods of prayer have proved of countless value to
many thousands, all the world over, it might be profitable to quote one passage which reveals his approach
to prayer.

> The second method of prayer consists in this; that the
> person, kneeling or sitting, according as he finds him-
> self more disposed, and as greater devotion accompanies
> him, keeping his eyes shut or fixed on one spot, without
> allowing them to wander about, should say the word
> Pater and dwell on the consideration of this word so
> long as he finds meanings, comparisons, relish and con-
> solation in thoughts about this word; and let him act in
> the same way in regard to each word of the Lord's
> prayer or of any other prayer whatsoever which he
> wishes to use for this method.

> The second rule is, that if a person considering the
> Lord's prayer, find in one or two words good matter for
> thought and spiritual relish and consolation, he should
> not be anxious to pass on, even though the hour be spent
> on that one word which he has found; and the time
> being finished let him say the rest of the Lord's prayer
> in the usual way.

Elsewhere St Ignatius writes:

> The fourth note is to enter into contemplation at one
> time kneeling, at another prostrate on the earth, or

M

stretched on the ground with my face upwards, now
seated, now standing, ever intent on seeking that which
I desire. Two things are to be noticed; first, if kneeling
or prostrate, I find that which I want, I will not try any
other position; secondly that in the point in which I
shall find what I desire, there will I rest, without being
anxious to proceed to another, until I have satisfied
myself.[4]

I find considerable satisfaction in quoting these two
great men together, for both at the time were laymen,
neither, at the time, was thought a mystic, and each in
his way achieved through prayer massive and heroic
results. They were middle-aged. They came to their
inner method of prayer through spiritual reading for
Ignatius was converted through reading the Gospel
story while More added to this an astonishing attach-
ment to the psalms. There is encouragement in the fact
that these two middle-aged men of the world were not
ashamed in private to adopt the posture of Moses, who
fell flat on his face before the burning bush.

Whatever the posture for our private prayer—and I
do beg you not to be too self-conscious or Anglo-Saxon
—it will be the odd word, whispered for hours, which
will open the door to our inner life. The transition from
prayer in private to inward prayer is the change from
thought to a yearning coloured by thought. A few
simple words, often repeated, serve as a bridge.

As we grow into middle age, we become less and less
able to think for long without restlessness and in-
attention but our longing for God increases day by
day. It is, therefore, important for us to consider this
question of words. We cannot forget that Christ himself, speaking of prayer, explicitly warned us against the

use of many words. His model prayer contains no long words and no involved expressions; each clause is but an explanation of the opening phrase. So Ignatius could suggest an hour and more on the words "Our Father", while Teresa devoted one whole section of a book to this one theme. If our spiritual reading is devoted to fashioning this awareness of God's tie with us, we, too, will pass from thought to desire without anxiety or strain.

Thomas More and Ignatius of Loyola give us all that we need to know about solitude and posture and the unknown author of *The Cloud of Unknowing* adds a most quaint but helpful note on the use of words. He writes, speaking of our yearnings for God and our inner aspirations:

> And if they be in words, as they be but seldom, then be they in full few words; yea and the fewer the better. Yea, and if it be but a little word of one syllable, methinks it is better than two, and more according to the work of the spirit. . . . A man or a woman affrighted by any sudden chance of fire or of a man's sudden death, or whatever else it be, suddenly in the height of his spirit, he is driven in haste and in need to cry or to pray for help. Yea how? Surely not in many words nor yet in one word of two syllables. And why is that? Because he thinketh it over long tarrying for to declare the need and the work of his spirit. And therefore be bursteth up hideously with a great spirit and cryeth but one little word of one syllable; such as this word Fire or this word Out. . . . And therefore it is written that short prayer pierceth heaven.[5]

Our author is here more concerned with method than with time. The length of our prayer is less his concern than the length and the shortness of our words. Time has no place in the prayer of the heart, for the surrender in our hearts to this deep and fundamental longing cannot be measured by the clock. Two seconds may seem to last for half an hour, nor can we count them until our heart is back to earth again. Indeed it usually happens that the moment that we are conscious that we are thus praying, the prayer is over and we must resume our thought and spiritual reading again.

I take time over this inward prayer for to many middle-aged people it becomes more and more natural, more and more satisfying, as soon as it is recognized for what it is. One must see it as a natural development, the growth of prayer from seed. For you may recall that in an earlier chapter, when we were considering our human make-up, the Ego, searching restlessly for completion and satisfaction, turns the light of consciousness over our unconscious mental states. Stored in us somewhere are the essences of past experience. Somehow we are able to evoke the essences of past friendships, past love, past satisfaction, past success. Unconsciously we somehow discard the shams, sift what was lasting from the temporary and ephemeral and build up a store of changeless satisfaction and security which books and art and friendship have contributed. St Francis de Sales compares this work of ours to the work of bees, collecting pollen from many different flowers, and St Augustine in a passage of unparalleled boldness thus describes a whole lifetime of spiritual activity.

Speaking to God, Augustine puts the question:

What is it that I love when I love thee? Not the beauty of any bodily thing nor the order of the seasons, nor the

brightness of light that rejoices the eye, nor the sweet
melodies of all songs, nor the fragrance of flowers and
ointments and spices; nor manna nor honey, not limbs
that carnal love embraces. None of these things do I love
in loving my God. Yet in a sense I do love light and
melody and fragrance and food and embrace when I love
my God;—the light and the voice and the fragrance and
food and the embrace in the soul when that light shines
upon my soul which no place can contain, that voice
sounds which no time can take away, I breathe a fragrance which no wind scatters, I eat the food which is not
lessened by the eating and I lie in the embrace which
satiety never comes to sunder. This it is that I love when
I love my God.

When we read such a passage as this in youth, we
admire it and dismiss it as lovely poetry; as we grow
older we grasp that poetry shrouds both reality and
truth: unless we are like poor Archie whose memories
of God were cold and artificial, unless we are like that
little girl playing in her doll's house for whom God is
the pale God of a subjective world. The more we read
Augustine's words, the more we sense the urgency of
that sensitive awareness, an awareness that while we are
gazing up to heaven, the lake is rising through the grass.

On the spiritual plane it is abundantly clear that no
human soul, by any device, can break the barrier of the
senses to penetrate beyond this central darkness and
obscurity. Some imaginative souls in every age have
sought to do so, often with disastrous results. In the
centre of our hearts we see nothing, hear nothing, surrender only to the dictates of that profound yearning
which motivates our lives. St Thomas More in his translation of the life of Pico della Mirandola expresses in

his majestic English all that we have been considering
here.

> When I stir thee to prayer, I stir thee not to the
> prayer that standeth in many words but to that prayer
> which, in the secret chambers of the mind, in the privy-
> closet of the soul with very affect speaketh unto God,
> and in the most lightsome darkness of contemplation not
> only presenteth the mind to the Father, but also uniteth
> it with Him by unspeakable ways, which they only
> know that have assayed. Nor care I not how long or how
> short thy prayer be but how effectual, how ardent. . . .
> Let no day pass, then, but thou once at the leastwise
> present thyself to God in prayer, and falling down be-
> fore Him flat to the ground.

The phrase "the most lightsome darkness of con-
templation" perfectly expresses the comfort of this
obscurity. It would be sad if we failed to recognize such
a state, such a method of prayer, such a surrender, if
we came to confuse such familiarity with slackness,
such silence with distraction, such union with presumption, such freedom from thought with loss of faith. For
here, in one form or another, is the prayer of the
middle-aged man, especially of those who have become aware of the beauty and of the love of the world
outside themselves. Here is a mystery which is also a
challenge, for the intensity of this craving which will
one day reach to heaven is, in large measure, determined over a lifetime by the effort that we have made
to forget ourselves.

Here in this mature and middle-aged prayer we find
the answer to the Noonday Devil and a peace which we
could never have known in youth. The signs of this
prayer are unusual and unmistakable. First the general

diminishing of thought, the satisfaction with a few words, the release from words, the sudden awareness of reality, profound, unchanging, in the very centre of the heart.

Should this prayer go further, as it so often does, then it turns into the kind of prayer described by St Teresa as "an interior recollection felt in the soul which seems to have acquired new senses, corresponding to its exterior senses and appears desirous of withdrawing from outward tumult. Consequently it sometimes carries the exterior senses away with it, being anxious to close its eyes so that it may neither hear nor see nor understand anything but what is then occupying it— namely the possibility of converse with God alone."[6]

The mystics take over at the very hint of such a possibility and I, in a flurry of emotion, end my little book. As Teresa puts it, "though not a word can be heard, either exteriorly or interiorly, the soul knows with perfect clearness who is there, where he is and sometimes what is signified by his presence. Whence he comes or how, she cannot tell but so it is, and for as long as it lasts she cannot cease to be aware of the fact."

Now you will grasp why I have so often emphasized this awareness. "Are you aware that we are drowning? The lake is rising through the grass."

NOTES

1. William James, *The Varieties of Religious Experience* (The Fontana Library). James was a deeply religious man though not officially denominational. One of the first of the great modern psychologists, he was invited to deliver the Gifford lectures in Edinburgh in 1901-1902 and the present book came as a result of these. He quotes Marcus Aurelius and gives the references, p. 60. I do not accept all his statements but his is a very profound and informative book.

2. Dr George Lawton's article was synopsized in the *Reader's Digest*, 1955.

3. Group Captain Leonard Cheshire tells his story in *Face of Victory* (Hutchinson, 1961); Douglas Hyde in *I Believed* (Heinemann, 1950).

4. Rudolf Allers, *Difficulties in Life* (Mercier Press, 1947). Allers is a well-known Catholic psychiatrist, Professor of Psychology in the Catholic University of America. Personally I found his book most helpful, many years ago. It seems less helpful now but he may hardly be blamed for that. I quote from p. 37.

5. Aldous Huxley, *The Perennial Philosophy* (Chatto & Windus, 1957). Huxley was, in my time, a University idol. I read the first edition of *The Perennial Philosophy* in 1946. It thrilled me then. As an anthology it cannot be bettered and Huxley's comments are a masterpiece. Somehow the book now no longer pleases me but I owe to it a massive debt. Is the author too certain of himself? The passages which he quotes are always delightful and

his deductions are penetrating without carrying the conviction which they once had. I quote from Chapter 9, p. 185.

6. *The Confessions of St Augustine.* Here we have one of the most remarkable books ever written, a book which, after many readings, has still not fully surrendered its inestimable appeal. Useless to hurry when reading it. I have used both the traditional text (Fontana Books, 1960) and the more readable but less artistic version by Frank Sheed (Sheed & Ward, 1943). Sheed knew what he was doing and he took the trouble to translate afresh because Augustine fills an urgent modern need. Sheed gives the final chapters which the traditional version omits. I quote from the Sheed edition. Augustine deals with the memory in Book Ten.

CHAPTER 2

1. St Teresa of Avila, *The Interior Castle.* I quote throughout from the Allison Peers translation (Sheed & Ward, 1946). St Teresa needs no introduction or impertinent praise. She enjoys some of the unction of the Scriptures and one has only to read her for a few moments to love God the more. Nevertheless, she is not always suitable as a guide. She is often hard to follow and because she is able to write with so much ease about such profound subjects, she puts strange ideas into some stupid people's heads. The fault is not hers. She describes the Interior Castle p. 202 and on p. 207 deals with the palmito. Augustine gives his description in the *Confessions*, Book X, VIII. Eckhart is quoted by Huxley, *op. cit.*, p. 186.

2. Dr F. Sherwood Taylor, M.A., B.Sc., Ph.D., wrote his fascinating little book *Two Ways of Life* in 1947 (Burns & Oates). He was an extraordinary man, a distinguished scientist, a convert to Catholicism who had in him both the precision of his calling and the warmth of his new-found faith. I quote from Chapter 3, pp. 35-36.

3. St Francis de Sales, *The Love of God*. The new and excellent translation by Fr Vincent Kerns was published by Burns & Oates (Orchard Series, 1962). St Francis is quite the most benign, whimsical and sympathetic of guides. Alas, he is now, also, very much dated, moving as he did in the slightly artificial society of seventeenth-century France. His letters are far more easy to read than his books. St Francis discusses the levels of the soul in Bk I, Chs. XI, XII. Indeed one must read the whole book. Yet Sherwood Taylor is, perhaps, far better suited to the bustle of our age.

4. The quotations from Alphonse Daudet are taken from William James, *op. cit.*, p. 173. His own views on the psychology of conversion I take from Lecture 9, pp. 194-201. I was aware that many new systems and explanations claim to have outdated James. This may well be. After reading a number, I found myself still very well satisfied with his.

5. The Newman quotation is from the *Development of Doctrine*, Ch. 1.

6. The lovely sonnet by Siegfried Sassoon is taken from his *Collected Poems* (Faber, 1947).

7. This text is from Luke 6.45, and "Where thy treasure is . . .", quoted later, from Matthew 6.21. I do not propose to give all the Gospel references.

CHAPTER 3

1. The examples here mentioned from the lives of various saints may be checked in almost any standard biography. St Teresa wrote her Autobiography and, in a sense, so did St Ignatius of Loyola who dictated many facts of his early life to a secretary. Here is a most revealing document, not now well known. The Autobiography of St Ignatius was published in 1900 (Benziger). He gives a full account of his scruples and the temptation to suicide, p. 48.

The Fénelon quotation is taken from Huxley, *op. cit.*, p. 292. The passage given by Huxley is a long one, dealing entirely with the great dangers of imagination.

2. Frank Sheed, *Theology and Sanity* (Sheed & Ward, 1948). This admirable book has helped thousands to a better understanding of their faith. The excellent quotations on the danger of imagination are taken from Chapter 2, p. 10, Ch. 3, p. 23. Also on the value of Christ's parables, p. 14.

3. There is no shortage of material about the harm done by the imagination. Perhaps the most outspoken attack is found in *The Cloud of Unknowing* (Burns & Oates, 1924), Ch. 65. Also on the imaginative picture of God and of the Angels, Ch. 57. See Note 5, Ch. 7.

CHAPTER 4

1. In this and in the following chapter, I have quoted at length from *Reason and Emotion* by Professor John Macmurray (Faber, 1962). The book was first published in 1935 and contained the lectures given at London University at about that date. This book has helped me more than I can say. It is a book which increases its hold on you yearly and never lets go. You and I may not agree with all that the Professor says. Yet his thought is penetrating and has coloured my whole approach. I quote from pp. 40-42, 100-101 and freely make use of Professor Macmurray's other thoughts. He, first, brought home to me the nature of Satan's lie in the Garden of Eden and the full meaning of St Paul's words. "I will know even as I am known". If I have unconsciously borrowed other ideas of his without acknowledgement, let him take this as a most sincere form of flattery. I wish I could agree with him in everything but he and I see differently about the Church.

2. C. S. Lewis, *The Problem of Pain* (Geoffrey Bles). Here is another book which has helped thousands and to which I am proud to offer my humble meed of praise.

I read it first in 1942 and many times since. With the *Screwtape Letters* and *Beyond Personality*, the *Problem of Pain* was a *must* in the preparation of this book. On the proofs of God's existence I refer to the very first page of the book, but do not be afraid to read on. After this book was completed, both C. S. Lewis and Aldous Huxley died. May I add a final note of gratitude to these two great men?

CHAPTER 5

1. Huxley's pointed words about charity may be found *op. cit.*, p. 97. I have more or less borrowed the paragraph from him.

2. I would not have dared to voice my opinion on the conviction that death cannot end true personal friendships had I not had the germ of the idea from the late Archbishop Alban Goodier, one time Archbishop of Bombay. This holy and distinguished man, whose *Life of Christ* is still so popular, not only spoke about this in public when I was present but practised it in his private life. When he himself was dead, I was astonished and overjoyed to find frequent references in his diaries to long conversations which he had with departed friends. There was, here, no question of spiritualist manifestations, for the Archbishop was a Preston Catholic of square-toed solidity. It was a question of faith. Among many other reasons for gratitude to this good man, I must place first this germ of an idea. It has been growing since 1933.

3. The young Pole is now Fr Thaddaeus Pelczar and when last I saw him, he came over from Chicago to meet me in Detroit. His was a wonderful lecture and it is a pleasure to acknowledge it.

CHAPTER 6

1. 'The Tyranny of the Should'. Though I do not quote this distinguished Anglo-American psychiatrist, I must pay my debt to Dr Karen Horney, M.D., for her development

of the Tyranny of the Should. You will find it in her *Neurosis and Human Growth* (Routledge, 1951), pp. 64-85. While, again, not accepting all her statements, I found her book most stimulating and profound. Among other of its most striking features is a wonderful working knowledge of great novels in which one may study faults of character.

3. Rudolf Allers, *op. cit.*, pp. 24f., discusses Christ's famous question about the speck in your brother's eye. Allers also deals with the misunderstandings possible in human speech.

2. I could not resist this second short quotation from Newman, less because he says here anything very positive but rather because his indignation is so final and so precise. In point of fact this quotation comes from his *Lectures on the Present Position of Catholics in England*, an amusing and fascinating book in which the whole notion of Prejudice is discussed most brilliantly.

CHAPTER 7

1. Our Lord's quoted sentence about secret prayer is found in Matthew 6.6.

2. *Thomas More.* His son-in-law William Roper is our authority for the new building. "And because he was desirous for godly purposes sometime to be solitary and sequester himself from worldly company, a good distance from his mansion house builded he a place called the New Building, wherein there was a chapel, a library and a gallery: in which, as his use was upon other days to occupy himself in prayer and study together, so on the Friday there usually continued he from morning till evening, spending his time only in devout prayers and spiritual exercises" (Roper, p. 80).

More was a remarkable man on many counts but the side of his life not yet fully developed is his method of prayer. Any study of his spiritual programme reveals (a) a deep appreciation of the liturgy; he served Mass daily; (b) constant spiritual reading as his *Dialogues* in the Tower of London testify; (c) an astonishing sense of humour, and this secret, inner life of prayer with God. Of course, as a boy he had been greatly drawn to the Carthusians.

Among the encouraging number of books about this most unusual Englishman, I myself prefer *St Thomas More* by E. E. Reynolds (Burns & Oates, 1953). It is from this book that I quote the glorious passage of the *Dialogues*, p. 334. Every life of More, contemporary or modern, provides a new aspect, but Reynolds seems to allow the saint more room to speak for himself.

3. Dom Bede Griffiths, *The Golden String* (Harvill Press, 1954). This book has been mentioned twice. To me it seems to be one of the most satisfying spiritual autobiographies attempted in our day. If St Francis de Sales is for the moment dated, Dom Bede Griffiths is certainly not.

4. The quotations from St Ignatius are taken from *The Text of the Spiritual Exercises* (Second English Edition, Burns & Oates, 1893), pp. 80, 29. A fine new translation of this extraordinary little book was published by Fr Thomas Corbishley (Burns & Oates, 1963) two days after this text was completed.

5. *The Cloud of Unknowing*. My quotation is taken from Chapter 37, p. 93. I have also had to borrow, along with so many others, the anonymous Englishman's phraseology. His is an amazing treatise on prayer, in one way comparable to the *Confessions* of Augustine; not everyone will find it helpful, but here is a book which grows on you.

6. The quotations from St Teresa are taken from her sober accounts of her life of prayer, presented to her confessor, P. Rodrigo Alvarez, and now published in Vol. I of the Allison Peers translation, pp. 326, 327. The great saint will forgive me for having run the two accounts together; they were both written from Seville and in the same year.